Touching from a D

Touching from a Distance

Ian Curtis and Joy Division

DEBORAH CURTIS

faber and faber

First published in Great Britain in 1995
by Faber and Faber Limited
3 Queen Square London WC1N 3AU
First published in this edition in 2001

Printed in England by Clays Ltd, St Ives plc

A CIP record for this book
is available from the British Library

ISBN 0–571–20739–1

2 4 6 8 10 9 7 5 3 1

WHEN ROUTINE BITES HARD, AND
AMBITION IS LOW,
AS RESENTMENT SETS IN, AND
EMOTIONS WON'T GROW,
AND WE'RE CHANGING TOO FAST,
TAKING OPPOSITE ROADS.

THIS BEDROOMS SO COLD, TURNED
AWAY ON YOUR SIDE,
IS MY TIMING SO FLAWED, ~~OUR RESPECT~~ OUR RESPECT HAS WORN DRY
~~THOUGH~~ THERE'S STILL THIS ~~WHY IS~~ APPEAL,
THAT WE'VE KEPT THRU OUR LIVES,

CRY OUT IN YOUR SLEEP, ALL MY
FAILINGS EXPOSED,
TASTE IN MY MOUTH, DESPERATION
TAKES HOLD,
JUST THAT SOMETHING SO GOOD,
CAN'T FUNCTION NO MORE.

Ian Curtis's original lyrics for 'Love Will Tear Us Apart'.

With love to Natalie

CONTENTS

LIST OF ILLUSTRATIONS

All uncredited photographs © Deborah Curtis.

ACKNOWLEDGEMENTS

A big thank you to all the people I interviewed: Iris Bates, Ernest Beard, Derek Brandwood, Kelvin Briggs, Oliver Cleaver, Steve Doggart, Franck Essner, Peter Hook, Michael Kelly, Terry Mason, Paul Morley, Stephen Morris, Tony Nuttall, Patrick O'Connor, Lindsay Reade, Peter Reid, Richard Searling, Bernard Sumner, Sue Sumner, John Talbot, Anthony Wilson and Helen Atkinson Wood.

Special thanks to Peter Bossley for his guidance and encouragement, without which I would still be grinding my teeth in my sleep!

Kisses to Wesley.

FOREWORD

Ian Curtis was a singer and lyric writer of rare, mediumistic power: his songs and performances for Joy Division conveyed desperate, raging emotions behind a dour, Mancunian façade. There were four in Joy Division – Curtis, Bernard Sumner, Peter Hook and Stephen Morris – but Ian was their eyes and ears: it was he who propelled them into uncharted territory – songs like 'Dead Souls' which, cold as the grave, has the infinity of a Gustave Doré hell.

It's easy to forget, now that Manchester is an international music city, just how isolated Joy Division were. At a time when the main venue of communication was the weekly music press, Joy Division shunned interviews: they survived and prospered through concerts, badges, seven-inch singles and word of mouth. During their last six months, the modern youth media began: style magazines like *The Face* and *i-D*, access programmes like *Something Else*, which Joy Division hi-jacked with a manic performance of 'She's Lost Control'.

Joy Division were not punk but they were directly inspired by its energy. Like punk, they used pop music as the means to dive into the collective unconscious, only this was not Dickensian London, but De Quincey's Manchester: an environment systematically degraded by industrial revolution, confined by lowering moors, with oblivion as the only escape. Manchester is a closed city, Cancerian like Ian Curtis: he remains the city's greatest song poet, capturing its space and its claustrophobia in a contemporary Gothick.

Manchester is also a big soul town: you breathe in black American dance music with the damp and pollution. Asked to write a song based on N. F. Porter's Northern Soul classic, 'Keep On Keeping On', Joy Division took the orginal's compulsive riff and blasted off into another dimension: 'Trying to find a way, trying to find a way – to get out!' Despite the dark lyric, traces of the original's hard-bitten joy and optimism come through, like a guide track erased in the finished master.

I was living in Manchester then, a Londoner transplanted to the North West; Joy Division helped me orient myself in the city. I saw this new environment through their eyes – 'Down the dark street, the houses look the same' – and felt it through the powerful atmosphere they generated on records and in concert. Their first album, *Unknown Pleasures*, released in June 1979, defined not only a city but a moment of social change: according to writer Chris Bohn, they 'recorded the corrosive effect on the individual of a time squeezed between the collapse into impotence of traditional Labour humanism and the impending cynical victory of Conservatism'.

Live, Joy Division rocked, very hard, but that was not all. Ian Curtis could give performances so intense that you'd have to leave the hall. Most performers hold something back when they're in front of an audience: what is called stagecraft or mannerism is, in fact, necessary psychic self-protection. Flanked by his anxious, protective cohorts – Bernard Sumner and Peter Hook – Ian Curtis got up, looked around and surrendered himself to his visions. This was not done in the controlled environment of a concert hall or studio, but in tiny, ill-equipped clubs which could at any moment explode into violence.

When you're young, death often isn't part of your world. When Ian Curtis committed suicide in May 1980, it was the first time that many of us had had to encounter death: the result was a shock so profound that it has become an unresolved trauma, a rupture in Manchester's social history which has persisted through the city's worldwide promotion as Madchester, and through the continuing success of New Order, the group formed by Joy Division's remaining trio. As Curtis himself sang on 'Komakino': 'Shadow at the side of the road / Always reminds me of you.'

Deborah Curtis was the last person to see her husband alive: at the most basic level, her memoir is the exorcism of the loss, guilt and confusion that followed his act of violence in their Macclesfield home. It tells us also about what has been much rumoured but never known: the emotional life of this most private of men. Much of the information in this book is printed here for the first time – an act of revelation that shows how deep the need is to break the bonds of Mancunian taciturnity.

It also tells us something that is ever present but rarely discussed: the role of women in the male, often macho, world of rock. Deborah Curtis is the wife who supported her husband, but who got left behind. There's a chilling scene where, heavily pregnant, Deborah goes to a Joy Division concert, only to be frozen out by an associate because she is not glamorous enough, because, in her own words, 'how.can we have a rock star with a six-months-pregnant wife standing by the stage?' And so, the cruelties begin.

There is another question which this book raises, as chilling as it is unanswerable. Deborah Curtis writes about the reality behind the persona, the fact that Ian Curtis had a condition – epilepsy – which was worsened by the exigencies of performance. Indeed, his mesmeric stage style – the flailing arms, glossy stare and frantic, spasmodic dancing – mirrored the epileptic fits that he had at home, that struck a chill into his intimates. Did people admire Ian Curtis for the very things that were destroying him?

I applaud Deborah Curtis's courage in writing this book, and believe that it will help to heal this fifteen-year-old wound. It may also help us to understand the nature of the obsession that continues to stalk rock culture: the romantic notion of the tortured artist, too fast to live, too young to die. This is the myth that begins with Thomas Chatterton and still carries on, through Rudolf Valentino, James Dean, Sid Vicious, Ian Curtis and Kurt Cobain. *Touching from a Distance* shows the human cost of that myth.

Jon Savage

1995

I wish I were a Warhol silk screen
Hanging on the wall
Or little Joe or maybe Lou
I'd love to be them all
All New York city's broken hearts
And secrets would be mine
I'd put you on a movie reel
And that would be just fine

*St Valentine's Day poem
from Ian to Debbie, 1973*

It was small and wrapped from head to toe in dirty rags, swaddled like a new-born baby. It was suspended from the telegraph pole and fluttered in the breeze before sailing gently down. Like an autumn leaf, it landed softly in the brook and its streamlined shape was taken quickly on the surface of the water, disappearing into the distance. I squeezed my whole body to scream but on waking all I could hear were my own muffled sobs.

My small daughter cuddled closer and tried to comfort me: 'Don't cry Mummy. Don't cry.'

My own mother opened the door and in the bar of light she was able to see which one of us was crying.

INTRODUCTION

On Friday 20 November 1992 Rebecca Boulton rang me from Rob Gretton's office and left a grave-voiced message on my answerphone. I shed tears when I heard that Factory Communications was going into receivership. To me, Ian Curtis *was* Factory, his company, his dream. They were tears of sorrow and relief.

Receivers Leonard Curtis and Partners held a meeting for unsecured creditors at noon on Monday 22 February 1993. The outcome was as expected: unsecured creditors would receive nothing. The directors of the company were Christopher Smith, Alan Erasmus and Anthony Wilson. Anthony Wilson, Alan Erasmus, Peter Saville and Rob Gretton were shareholders. None of them attended the meeting.

As Ian's beneficiary I was asked to go to London to sign my part in a contract with London Records. After months of negotiating, Rob Gretton had the unenviable task of persuading New Order and myself to sign on the dotted line with him as manager once more. I caused him some consternation by saying I needed to read and understand the thing first, though I didn't cause as much anxiety as Bernard Sumner, who initially refused to get out of bed!

On 23 December 1992, twenty years to the day since Ian first asked me out, I boarded the train at Macclesfield. There was Rob, as bearlike as ever, waving me down to first class. As I sat, he explained that first class was a must if he wanted to smoke in peace. I felt in my bag for my asthma medication and tried to relax. The conversation was stilted to begin with. We had exchanged bitter words in the past, but Rob does not appear to hold grudges. He explained that he was not even sure if Bernard would turn up. I realized that my own reluctance to abandon my other responsibilities and jump on a train to

London two days before Christmas was but a small hiccup. Rob had already declined to be interviewed for my book and I was not prepared to push him. Though he has remained a friend, we keep a respectful distance, preferring not to discuss Ian. Yet he speaks freely of the problems he has had with New Order. There are tales of petty jealousy, time-wasting arguments and discontentment. But he's not complaining, he's smiling. This stress-beleaguered, slow-talking man has enjoyed it!

> 'In a way I've grown away from the other members of the band, but I think anyone who's together for that amount of time eventually needs a bit of distance. It's only natural.'
>
> Bernard Sumner

When we arrived at Polygram, Bernard was already there. He had flown down ahead of us and was in Roger Ames's office 'having words'. Eventually we trooped into the room where the contract was being combed through by solicitors Iain Adam, James Harman and John Kennedy. Bernard sat next to me because he and I were the non-smokers. Little good this did him – the others puffed away as if their lives depended upon it. When it became clear that the contract wasn't ready, we adjourned to the pub with Marcus Russell, Electronic's manager, and Tracy Bennett, Roger Ames's successor. If I had given someone else power of attorney, I would have been spared the trip but, understandably, I was not prepared to do this. Peter Hook was supposedly mid-air between Los Angeles and London while someone else signed temporarily for him. Steve Morris and Gillian Gilbert were extracted from a bar in the Seychelles for last-minute telephone negotiations. And listening to Bernard in the pub, I thought there was no way that he was going to sign.

By the time we did sign, you could have cut up the smoke in the office along with the atmosphere and given everyone a piece to take home. If I ever thought that signing a contract with a major record company would be exciting, I was mistaken. There was no real euphoria from any of the parties concerned and I couldn't help feeling as if I had been kept behind for detention. I stood in the frosty air outside while Rob politely tried to locate Roger Ames to say good-bye and thank him, but Roger was nowhere to be seen. There were bomb scares all over London and little time to spare before the last train back to Manchester. At Euston Station we were evacuated for yet another alert. Then the train was diverted and was so late that British Rail felt obliged to offer us a stiff drink.

When Ian and his friends were young they all talked about how they were going to move to London. Most of them did. Tony Nuttall teaches graphic design, Oliver Cleaver is a high-powered advertising executive and Helen Atkinson Wood is a successful actress. Ironically, one way or another Ian had 'gone to London' too. After hugging Rob, I stepped off the train at Macclesfield. It was very late and extremely cold. For a moment I felt lonely, as if I had left someone or something behind – the widow again. And while sometimes I can't help looking over my shoulder and remembering when we were young, in my heart I know that forward is the only real direction. The signing with London Records released me from my past; I finally felt justified in completing my tale and allowing Ian to rest.

CHAPTER ONE

AN URBAN SOUNDTRACK

Ian Kevin Curtis was born in the Memorial Hospital, Old Trafford, Manchester, on St Swithin's Day, 15 July 1956, although at the time his parents, Kevin and Doreen Curtis, lived in Hurdsfield on the out-skirts of Macclesfield. They had been married four years and Kevin was a Detective Officer in the Transport Commission Police. The small family unit was close knit, and Ian and his younger sister Carole spent much of their childhood visiting relatives in Man-chester. Ian had fond childhood memories of the time spent with his mother's parents and often spoke of more distant relatives who lived in Canvey Island, Essex.

Even at pre-school age, Ian showed a love of books and a keenness to learn. His favourite stories were those in his treasured collection of Ladybird history books. He particularly liked to draw Roman sol-diers and gladiators and as soon as he was old enough began to lap up films such as *El Cid* and *Jason and the Argonauts*. As an infant he attended Trinity Square Primary School in Macclesfield where he was considered a delightful child to teach, after which he went to Hurdsfield Junior School.

The Curtis family became particularly friendly with the Nuttalls who lived five doors up from them on Balmoral Crescent. The two mothers were constant companions and, as a result, Ian's closest friend for the next sixteen years was Tony Nuttall. Tony was wiry and eighteen months younger than Ian, and they were nicknamed Batman and Robin. Despite being in different years at primary school, they always met at the gate and ran home for dinner together. Indulging in all the usual street games, they played spies and bandits and tried to keep in with the big boys, choosing to like the Who and the Rolling Stones because it was considered more manly than liking the Beatles.

Ian inherited his father's love of writing and silent moods. Kevin Curtis had written several plays, but they had never been published. One of Ian's favourite relatives was his father's sister, Aunty Nell, a large, overbearing woman with an excessive determination to get what she wanted from life. Bold and generous, Aunty Nell showered Ian with gifts and transfixed him with tales of her youth and her early modelling career. She made her life seem so exciting and instilled in him a great belief that there was more to living than working nine to five and sharing an identical existence to your neighbours. Their personalities were strikingly similar in that they were both self-assured and determined, although sometimes it seemed as if Nell would actually lend some of her confidence to Ian – he was visibly more outgoing in her company. As she had no children of her own she tended to mother him a little and often their relationship would appear slightly conspiratorial. One had the impression that if Ian were to confide in anyone, it would be Aunty Nell.

Her father, Grandfather Curtis, is recalled by Ian's family as a 'wonderful old fellow' who died with barely a penny in his pocket, but Ian would romanticize and describe an Irish man who changed his religion every day and joked about the Irish political situation. Grandfather Curtis came from Port Arlington which is now in County Kildare, twenty-seven miles from Dublin. In 1900 he and his brother joined the army and went out to India for twelve years. Ian's grandfather loved India and the army life, so it is not surprising that although he was demobbed just as the First World War was starting, he re-enlisted immediately and joined the Royal Horse Artillery in France. Despite being wounded, he survived the war and returned not to Ireland but to England, where his parents had settled. An avid reader of non-fiction, his insatiable interest in the world around him and his exciting lifestyle made him a captivating companion for Ian. The two of them spent a great deal of time talking together and his grandfather's death when Ian was only seven years old left a large hole in the young boy's life. Ian often spoke of the jocular granddad who was a loser at cards, but had the charming good looks of Errol Flynn.

Ian was a performer from a very early age and seemed to be forever taking his fantasies to the extreme. Once, when he had decided to be a stunt man, he persuaded Tony to help him rig up a wooden sledge as a landing pad. After drumming up local children to watch, he donned an old crash-helmet and jumped from the roof of a one-storey garage. The sledge shattered in all directions and the showman walked away from his first stunt.

Ian never did anything by halves; any interest became a vocation. Speedway rider Ivan Majors was Ian's hero and he drew parallels between himself and the dashing world champion, dubbing his friend Tony as a new Chris Pusey – a less glamorous, stubbly chinned rider, who was renowned for crashing. When they were in their early teens the boys saved £10 and bought an old BSA Bantam motorcycle. They knew nothing about engines and after pushing the bike five miles home, congratulated themselves on using second gear in the fields. Ian was not mechanically minded, not really relishing getting his hands dirty. He always had a fascination for fame and the glamorous side of life, but the practical considerations that go with it escaped him. When he was older he would speak of owning a prestigious car, yet he shied away from learning to drive.

Ian took his hobbies very seriously. Rather than just kick a ball around the field with a few friends he organized a football team called the Spartans – his childhood admiration for the Ancient Greeks helped him to choose the name. He arranged fixtures by advertising in a magazine. His approach was always to decide how best to get something done; failure was not an option. Ian appeared to get what he wanted and Tony Nuttall could never decide if Ian was spoilt or whether he was able to make things happen through sheer determination. Either way, he was always able to find the initiative when he wanted something badly.

The first band Ian formed was with Tony Nuttall, Peter Johnson and Brian McFaddian. Peter wore his spectacles on the end of his nose and was considered respectable and studious. He played the

3

piano in a radical way by plucking the strings with a pencil. Later he went to the King's School with Ian, where he became interested in classical music. Brian was a guitarist whom Ian and Tony had met while caddying for pocket money at Prestbury golf club. Ian chose to play bass and Tony bought himself a drum kit. Very young and obviously ahead of their time, Ian's first band died an apparently painless death shortly thereafter.

In the late 1960s, the large community of back-to-back terraced houses behind Macclesfield railway station was demolished to make way for a new complex of council flats. Each block was indistinguishable from the next. With their long, shared balconies and lonely stairways, they were destined to become more insalubrious than the housing they replaced. Unaware of their impending fate, the Curtis family were pleased to be allocated a flat overlooking the football field. With a pleasant view and in close proximity to Macclesfield town centre the new flat seemed ideal. They left their comfortable house with a garden and friendly neighbours, and moved nearer to the town centre.

Ian began a new phase in his life when he passed his eleven-plus examination and was admitted to the King's School in Macclesfield. It was and still is a school with a good reputation, although intelligence is no longer the only entry requirement, and the cost today would be prohibitive to a typical working-class family.

Ian was understandably apprehensive about the type of people who would attend such a school. Socially it was a long way from his home in Victoria Park. Nevertheless, he soon made a very mixed bunch of friends. The first was Kelvin Briggs, whom he recognized from one of his football fixtures against a team from Adlington. A few of his new friends were to some extent rather plummy, but Ian remained unpretentious and did not try to blend in with them. He grew his hair longer than the others so that it was difficult to see his face. This may have been the intention as at this time his face was still chubby and his jowled appearance had earned him the nickname of 'Hammy'. He was also quite tall and his ubiquitous limbs were awkward, as if he didn't quite know what to do with them. Yet when he channelled his energy in the right direction, he was a competitive rugby player and enjoyed sprint training. Of course, this didn't prevent him skiving off lessons for the all-essential cigarette.

Most people felt either drawn to Ian or rejected by him, depending on how they interpreted his demeanour. He is described by Mike Kelly, a childhood acquaintance who lived nearby, as a person one would cross the road to avoid merely because his eyes said: 'Stay away.'

Oliver Cleaver found Ian intriguing, partly because of his background and image, but also because they shared the same view on the educational system at King's. They kicked against the rigidity of the school timetable, feeling that it discouraged individuality in its pupils. Part of Oliver's rebelliousness involved friendship with Ian. The two of them challenged the ritualistic life of the school whenever possible. Both Oliver's parents were teachers and Oliver's sister was at university reading Russian. The prospect of knowing Ian Curtis must have seemed like an ideal opportunity for Oliver to break away from his ordered and relatively safe life. However, Ian was always very well behaved when introduced to anyone's parents and came across as a quiet, serious young man. His recalcitrance could be well hidden when necessary.

Ian's main love in life was music and many lunchtimes were spent at the Victoria Park flat listening to the MC5, Roxy Music and the Velvet Underground. His fanaticism for David Bowie, and in particular his version of Jacques Brel's song 'My Death', was taken at the time to be a fashionable fascination and merely Ian's recognition of Bowie's mime, choreographed by Lindsay Kemp. The fact that most of Ian's heroes were dead, close to death or obsessed with death was not unusual and is a common teenage fad. Ian seemed to take growing up more seriously than the others, as if kicking against it could prolong his youth. He bought a red jacket to match the one James Dean wore in *Rebel Without a Cause*. He wanted to be that rebel but, like his hero, he didn't have a cause either. Mostly his rebellion took the form of verbal objection to anyone else's way of life and, if he thought it appropriate, a sullen or disinterested expression. Because he was different, people wanted to be included in his circle of friends. He could draw in a person with his enigmatic charisma, which even then was obvious.

It was impossible for Ian to afford the albums he wanted as well as cigarettes and drink, so it wasn't long before he resorted to going to the indoor market in Macclesfield wearing a great coat. Records stolen beneath the coat one week would be resold to the same stall a week later. Ian and his school friends would often visit an off-licence, stuffing small bottles of spirits up their jumpers before the little old lady came out to sell them a Mars bar. Ian's actions were always more considered, he never took any real risks, while Oliver always felt that if he got into serious trouble his family would be there to fall back on. Ian was less blasé, possibly because his father was a policeman, but he enjoyed flirting with authority. He relished choosing outrageous clothes, perhaps wearing something in heinous taste and with eye make-up to draw attention to himself. He and Tony Nuttall would go for an under-age drink at the Bate Hall in Macclesfield because the local CID drank there. Sometimes during school lunch hours, Ian would visit The Bull in Victoria Park flats with his King's School friends. They would take off their school ties and chat up the girls, thinking they were men of the world with their half pints of lager. Kelvin remembers being caught in a pub leading to a one-week suspension from school, but fortunately he was able to intercept the letter that the school wrote to his parents.

Ian and his contemporaries were able to smoke dope, sniff solvents and still leave time for studies. Although it was obvious to his friends that Ian was clever, he never seemed to do any work. His studies may have suffered, but he still managed to gain seven O levels in English Language, English Literature, Religious Knowledge, History, Latin, French and Mathematics. He was even awarded prizes in his favourite subjects – History and Divinity. Ironically, despite his admiration of the pomp and power of Germany, he failed O level German. He never spoke about furthering his education or which university he would like to attend. Although it was seldom discussed, the other boys had realistic career plans, but Ian always talked of a career in the music business. He and Oliver would bicker about who would be the singer in the band, but Oliver never took the conversations seriously. It was clear to Oliver that groups such as the Beatles became famous in the music business by practising laboriously. No one ever saw Ian learning to play the guitar and he never stood up and sang. His posing antics in the bedroom were taken as part of the fun, not a serious commitment to stardom.

'It was a big leap for me to think beyond being a fan of the music and wanting to emulate the lifestyle of the performers. The kind of musicians we liked were on the fringes of normal life.'

Oliver Cleaver

When Mott the Hoople's 'All the Young Dudes' hit the charts, Ian began to use the lyrics as his creed. He would choose certain songs and lyrics such as 'Speed child, don't wanna stay alive when you're twenty-five', or David Bowie's 'Rock and Roll Suicide', and be carried away with the romantic magic of an early death. He idolized people like Jim Morrison who died at their peak. This was the first indication anyone had that he was becoming fascinated with the idea of not living beyond his early twenties, and the start of the glitter and glamour period in his life.

By 1972, taking easily available household drugs became a pastime taken for granted by Ian. Tony Nuttall was often included in these escapades, but was unable to take to some of Ian's new chums. Despite being friends for so long, they began to drift apart. This was exacerbated by the fact that Tony had failed his eleven-plus and attended a secondary modern school on the other side of town.

It was customary at the King's School for certain boys to do 'social services' on Wednesday afternoons. This involved either going to play bingo with the elderly people in their retirement homes, or visiting the more agile in their own homes or the alms houses where some of them lived. While playing bingo, Ian and his friends would sniff at their handkerchiefs which previously had been soaked in dry-cleaning fluid in an effort to make the afternoon more enjoyable. The old people found the boys very entertaining as they were so lively and laughed a great deal.

Visiting the homes of pensioners living alone was much more lucrative. One boy would keep the old person talking and the other would pretend to use the bathroom in order to steal any drugs left in the bathroom cabinet. On one particular occasion, Ian and Oliver managed to obtain some chlorpromazine hydrochloride (brand name Largactil) which was considerably more dangerous than what they had stolen previously. Unbeknown to them it is prescribed for schizophrenia and related psychoses, and the emergency control of behavioural disturbance. Its side effects include drowsiness, apathy, depression, agitation and blurred vision. The following Thursday, unable to face the prospect of double History, they each took three tablets.

This was a normal dose for the tablets they usually took, but the Largactil was stronger and something that they had not tried before. The teacher woke them up and they went off to separate lessons. Oliver's next lesson was Drama, but he was sent home because his tutor thought he was drunk. Ian was also sent home and there he gave Tony a couple of the tablets.

When Kevin Curtis returned to the flat he listened outside his son's bedroom and could hear nothing but the sound of a record clicking around the turntable. He banged on the door to wake them up. Tony was in a confused state, yet after trying to put on still more clothes over his jacket, he was able to walk home to Hurdsfield. Ian was taken to have his stomach pumped. On leaving the hospital Ian met Oliver, who was only just going in. He had gone straight to bed when he got home, but his mother was concerned. She had called a doctor who said that he did not know what was wrong with Oliver. By midnight, when she had trouble finding his pulse, she sent for an ambulance.

Ian said he had taken the tablets for a laugh to see what would happen. Oliver's explanation was more dramatic and with his tongue lodged firmly in his cheek he said flippantly that he was trying to kill himself. Sadly, Ian's welfare was forgotten and his more humorous

friend spent every Wednesday for the following six months having
counselling. There were repercussions at school, of course. Both of
them were suspended, Ian longer than Oliver for some reason. It may
have been Oliver's lie that prevented the boys from being expelled. In
the end it was Stephen Morris, in the year below Ian and Oliver at the
King's School, who was expelled for over-indulging in cough medi-
cine.

The stomach-pumping incident hadn't deterred Ian. Many more
lunchtimes were spent in Sparrow Park – an oasis of peace behind
the bustle of what used to be a market place, behind St Michael's
church in Macclesfield town centre – sniffing dry-cleaning fluid or
popping pills in relative seclusion.

Sometimes when Ian took his friends back to his parents' flat, he
would mime to records on his acoustic guitar. He had made a brief,
half-hearted attempt to learn to play, with little success. The drugs
they took dulled their senses and Ian would often inflict pain on himself to see how much he could bear in this anaesthetized state. He
used cigarettes to burn his skin and would hit his leg with a spiked
running shoe. His pals would laugh at the blood, but were never
inspired to copy him. Yet Ian's violence was not directed at anyone
else. Friends found him extremely loyal. He would decide whom he
was going to 'do right by' and stick to them. His stubborn streak
meant that he seldom changed his mind about a person.

I was six months younger than Ian and attended Macclesfield High
School for Girls, which was considered at the time to be a sister establishment to the King's School. I was born in Liverpool, but my parents left the city when I was three in order to bring up my younger
sister and me in a more rural and less fraught environment. After
spending a couple of years in Wiltshire and Sussex, we had finally
settled in Macclesfield, Cheshire.

The Victoria Park flats were situated half-way between Macclesfield High School and the bus station, so it became a habit for me and
my friends to stop off at the family advice centre there before catching the bus home. The centre and the youth club were run as a joint

venture and provided help and support for the residents of the council flats. An odd assortment of people would hang out there.

> 'We used to bounce between different groups of friends.
> Within each group there was a particular way you behaved.
> There was only one time I saw him in an extreme state of
> anxiety. One afternoon, me, Colin Hyde and Ian had taken a
> load of sulphate, which heightens your anxiety level, gives
> you a jittery anticipation. Staying together as a group was
> fine, we listened to records, etc. But then Colin and I had to
> go up to Hurdsfield and we left Ian on his own. When we
> were walking back down Park View corridor, we could see
> Ian pacing up and down in a manic way and he had a
> Hoover flexible hose wrapped around him. Anxiety was
> streaming out of him. His mum had come back and he
> couldn't stay in the house. He was wrapping it around him-
> self in a morose, jittery way – we thought it was a snake at
> first – and he had that drained look he sometimes got. It was
> a particular look, wasted, ashen. That was possibly the first
> time I had ever seen him with that expression.'
>
> Tony Nuttall

Sometimes the family advice centre provided a cover for truancy
which would otherwise have kept the local children on the streets, and
I suppose it gave them a shelter without question or interference.
Sometimes this went horribly wrong. On one occasion a group of
youngsters hid themselves in a store cupboard to sniff 'camping gaz'.
When the atmosphere became unbearable, Colin Hyde leapt out and
then tried to push the door closed on the others. Ian managed to struggle out, then Tony Nuttall, but Colin struck a match and threw it into
the cupboard before anyone else could leave. The three remaining
youngsters were lucky to escape with blistered faces and arms, and
singed hair.

That summer after Ian had taken his first overdose, I met Tony
Nuttall at the youth club. With his scruffy clothes, untidy hair and
long nose, he resembled a cross between a young Rod Stewart and
Cat Weasel, but his sense of humour and wide smile gave him an

attractive appeal all of his own. He spoke of his friend Ian and was so excited at the prospect of introducing me to him that, one evening, I agreed to leave the youth club with him. Ian was living at 11 Park View with his parents and sister. As we walked towards the end of the landing and rounded the corner, I saw a tall figure staring out over the balcony and across the football pitch. I was intrigued, though not drawn to him. His hair was quite long, he was wearing make-up and eye shadow and his sister's short pink fun-fur jacket. He nodded at me politely, but did not seem particularly interested in Tony's new girlfriend. I felt like I was at an audition or waiting to be granted an audience. I got to know Tony through the club, but despite the fact that he and Ian were such close friends, I never saw Ian there.

Over the following months I spent most of my spare time with Tony and Ian. Our usual meeting place was Mr and Mrs Curtis's flat. Although the other rooms were cosy, Ian's room looked like a cell and reflected Ian's minimalist attitude towards decor. There were two single beds – presumably for when Tony stayed the night – and a chest of drawers. Ian's record collection was neatly held in a small box and although his taste could be varied, he was in the habit of changing his discs rather than extending his collection. His other prized possessions, namely his *Oz* magazines and his collection of music newspapers, were in the bottom drawer of the chest. Most telling of all was a black ring-file holding lined paper and cardboard filing cards. Each filing card was labelled either 'Novel', 'Poems', or 'Songs'. I thought him rather ambitious, but he showed no signs of embarrassment about it.

Tony and I were rarely alone as a couple. When it was cold and wet, the three of us listened to records in Ian's bedroom and if Tony and I wanted a kiss and a cuddle, Ian would sit and smoke. I didn't notice Ian paying any particular attention to me and often wondered why he didn't find himself a girlfriend so that we could make up a foursome, but he seemed content to lie back with his cigarettes and listen to music. My own taste included the Beatles, Creedence Clearwater Revival, T Rex and the Love Affair (mainly because of my crush on lead singer Steve Ellis). Ian's was diverse and exciting, and quite different to the poppy Motown-type music that my friends were listening to.

These times were the best, as Tony and Ian didn't take drugs if they were spending the day with me, but quite often they played truant together and would meet me after school. Sometimes they took Valium purloined from someone's parents, or sniffed whatever toxic substance they could lay their hands on. Both their faces would be cold and pallid, and their breath heavy with the fumes of carbon tetrachloride.

> 'Taking Valium was meant to be fun. There was never anything sinister about it, but it got out of hand. That had a lot to do with this romantic image. Taking drugs seemed a good image. When I was told he had killed himself, my first thought was: "What an indulgent bastard he is." There was no need to do it. What he really wanted to do was play rock and roll. I think he was doing what he wanted to do. The theatrical way he did it suggests ... He did enjoy the theatre and he did enjoy his theatrics affecting other people. I think that was important to him. It wasn't enough to dress up and go out; he had to get drunk and wind people up. We all thought it was fun and it *was* fun to an extent. But it was an indulgence – you could only get away with it between certain years.'
>
> Tony Nuttall

Sometimes Ian would say he suffered 'flashbacks'. He described situations where he would have a sensation of floating, as if he had taken drugs when in fact he had not. This was always assumed to be a side effect of whatever he had taken the previous week. No one thought they might have been early epileptic fits. Either way, he would not have told his parents about it.

Events such as these were too easily passed off as the effects of drug abuse. We attended a small gig held in a hut next to the public library on Park Green, Macclesfield. The band playing used a strobe light while they were on stage and after watching it for a time, Ian collapsed on the floor. He was unceremoniously pulled out by the armpits, heels dragging, and left to recover in another room.

Eventually, Tony Nuttall and I parted company. At the time I was mystified. There was no big row, no confrontation, nothing. One day I was flavour of the month; the next I had time on my hands. Luckily, I was able to pick up where I had left off with my friends. I remember the summer of 1972 as long, hot and balmy. All my pocket money was spent on Loons, love beads and joss sticks.

The King's School had an innovative drama teacher called Graham Wilson. When putting together a production of Tom Stoppard's *The Real Inspector Hound*, he decided to ask if any Macclesfield High School girls would be interested in sharing the project. As these two schools were the grammar schools in Macclesfield, it was only natural that they should try out some joint ventures. It was during rehearsals for the play that Oliver Cleaver first met Helen Atkinson Wood, who was head girl of our school. Like me, she was told she just *had* to meet this boy called Ian Curtis who wore black nail varnish. Ian and Helen had backgrounds which were poles apart, but they developed a close friendship. When the lanky, awkward boy from the council flat met the petite, effervescent blonde, there was a mutual interest.

> 'There was always something that felt quite wicked about knowing Ian … He didn't really need to talk about it because he had that self-destruct part of his personality, but you don't even need to be talking about dangerous things, because you know that if somebody is actually doing that to themselves then they are looking for a different journey than perhaps the one you're looking for or perhaps the one that anyone that you know is.'
>
> Helen Atkinson Wood

Ian's interest in Helen stemmed neither from her status as head girl nor her wealthy background. He was fascinated by the fact that at sixteen she had fractured her skull when she fell off her horse. Helen was unconscious for three days and took two school terms to recover.

The idea of someone learning to speak, read, gain their memory and walk, let alone get back on the horse and ride again, made Helen all the more attractive to Ian. He embellished her story and retold it several times, which gave me a vision of Helen as Heidi's friend Clara. Helen puts it down to Ian's fascination with drama, but nonetheless his admiration for her obvious courage was central to their friendship. Helen was sure that the ordinary held no magic for Ian and, though he never actually said it outright, she suspected that he found the idea of dying young magic in itself and was not surprised when he carried it through.

On 23 December 1972, four of my friends – Gillian, Anne, Dek and Pat – decided to hire the Scout Hut on Fence Avenue and hold a double engagement party. Pat remembers Ian as a joking, laughing person to whom music was the only thing that really mattered. Ian rarely introduced his friends to his family. He would tear downstairs, push his friends into his room, lock the door and put the music on. Ian arrived at Pat's party in a stupor and confided to me that he had a bet on with his friends that he would be able to kiss the most girls that night. Consequently I spent the remainder of the evening introducing him to all of my school friends. Finding it very amusing, they all acquiesced.

Before we parted, Ian asked me to go out with him and invited me to a David Bowie gig at the Hard Rock in Manchester. What thrilled me was not particularly the opportunity of going out with Ian, but more the chance to get out of Macclesfield and to be included in a crowd of people who did more than catch the train to Stockport for a weekly shopping trip. I was looking forward to seeing Tony again, though I never got the chance to ask him why he dumped me so unceremoniously as he kept his distance.

Ian was a big Bowie fan and had already managed to spend time in his dressing room at one gig. He had David Bowie's, Trevor Boulder's and Mick Ronson's autographs, one of Woody's broken drumsticks and a spare guitar string. Bowie was playing for two nights and as Ian and Tony had tickets for both nights, Ian arranged for his friends to pick me up and take me to meet him for the second gig.

This was the first time I had been to a proper gig. I was even excited about the support band, Fumble. I loved their rendition of 'Johnnie B. Good', not realizing that every rock band covers that song. When Bowie emerged wearing a one-piece printed outfit that resembled a legless babygro, we all gazed up in complete adoration. The stage was so small that he was extemely close to the audience, yet no one dared to touch his skinny, boyish legs.

Ian had had only one serious girlfriend before me. Bev Clayton was tall and slim with large eyes and waist-length titian-coloured hair. Yet from that night on, I was Ian's girlfriend and stopped even looking at other boys. I felt honoured to be part of that small group. For a short time I did not regard Ian as an individual, but as a party of people who were fun and exciting and knew more than me about life itself. I didn't realize that Ian's King's School friends were also receiving their first introduction to David Bowie, Lou Reed and perhaps the seamier side of Ian's ethereal world.

I had attended primary school in the village of Sutton, in the hills of Macclesfield. My childhood weekends had been spent looking for birds' nests, building dams across the river Bollin, and feeding orphan lambs. By the time I met Ian, I had abandoned my push-bike and stopped attending the church youth club, but was still leading a quiet existence. Suddenly, life seemed one long round of parties, pop concerts and pub crawls. It was a whole new scene for me and, like Ian, I gradually began to move away from my old circle. Ian never hid his interest for stars who had died young. Through him I began to learn about James Dean, Jim Morrison and Janis Joplin. Anyone who had been involved in the young, arty medium of any form of showbusiness and found an early grave was of interest to him. When he told me that he had no intention of living beyond his early twenties, I took it with a pinch of salt, assumed it was a phase and that he would grow out of it. He seemed terribly young to have already made the decision that life was not worth living. I thought that, as he matured, surely life would be so good that he would not want to leave it all behind.

Gradually we began to see very little of Tony Nuttall. Ian admitted one day that Tony had agreed to let him date me on the condition that he looked after me. Though I felt like a pet with a new owner, my life was more interesting and somewhat more sophisticated with Ian, so I stuck with him.

Occasionally we put ourselves on the baby-sitting rota and looked after the children who lived in Victoria Park flats while their parents went out. This was by no means a mundane job. Once we cared for two small boys whose parents had recently settled down after working in a circus. There were circus posters on the walls and the children leapt around from one piece of furniture to another, like monkeys who had been let out of their cage. Another time a small girl climbed on to Ian's knee and asked him if he would be sleeping with her Mummy that night and whether he was her Daddy.

Ian somehow managed to balance his life between his council-estate friends and his more affluent peers at the King's School. I also tried to keep hold of my old friends, but I was not as successful, mainly because Ian strongly objected to them. Without me realizing it, he began to take control of my life very early on in our relationship.

My friend Elaine and I had Saturday jobs on a cheese and bacon stall in the indoor market in Macclesfield town centre. Ian wanted me to walk to his flat every lunch-time so that his mother could make me a sandwich. Instead of speaking up I allowed myself to be the victim of either Doreen's misplaced kindness or Ian's determination to keep tabs on me. He always met me and escorted me to and from the stall. Considering the time I spent at the flat, I rarely saw Ian's sister Carole. She was like Ian in appearance, but was always ready with a shy smile. She had not passed the eleven-plus to go to the local grammar school, so I assumed she was not as academically gifted as Ian. Although she was only about thirteen at the time, I once suggested to Ian that it would be nice when Carole started going out with boys so that we could make up a foursome. Ian replied, 'My sister's never going to go out with boys!'

Ian would often spoil a pleasant evening by having an inexplicable temper tantrum. When half a dozen of us visited a friend's home, one of us complimented our friend's father on his house. The embarrassed father blushed and spluttered a little before saying, in a self-effacing manner, 'It's better than living in Moss Side.' Ian immediately leapt upon his soap box and said, 'What's wrong with Moss Side?' While the poor man struggled to explain himself, Ian accused him of being racist, threw a punch at another guest and ended up crouching on the floor behind the settee. I remember kneeling down and trying to persuade him to come out, but he was as implacable as ever. Most probably it was Oliver Cleaver who eventually coaxed him into going home.

In the summer of 1973, Oliver's parents went away on holiday, leaving Oliver to stay at a friend's house. Oliver let us back into his parents' house and we had a small but out-of-hand party which came to an abrupt end when Ian smashed his fist through the glass in the front door. No one knew why he was so angry, but the wound could not have been very deep as we were able to walk to casualty.

Autumn arrived and life was in danger of becoming boring again. However, while Oliver was drinking at the Park Tavern, he struck up a friendship with Robert from Copperfield Antiques and John Talbot who toured the antiques fairs. They were in the habit of throwing parties rather more frequently than anyone else we knew and the atmosphere of those evenings will remain with me forever. One of the happiest times of my life ensued. An impressionable sixteen-year-old, with Keats's 'The Eve of St Agnes' ringing in my ears, I fantasized that one day we could all return to the days of wizards and knights in shining armour.

The antique shop was a listed building, barely in the town centre of Macclesfield. Each time we went to a party there, Ian tapped on the door and it was opened the smallest peep. For some reason I always anticipated rejection, but we were never refused admission. There would be a roaring coal fire in the grate, the firelight licking the stone walls and ancient paving stones, camp-sounding music and often something to eat. The food would be elaborately laid out like a feast, with a huge bowl of punch into which everyone poured whatever they had brought with them.

As the evening wore on, guests would disrobe and squeeze into the shower together. Ian was reluctant to join in with such antics – he was more likely to be found standing in a corner smoking. One evening a rather plain but nubile young girl slid naked between us while we were in one of the four-poster beds. Ian was horrified and kicked her out again. Yet Ian wasn't always opposed to the presence of other females. When he disappeared for a long time one night I asked Kelvin to find him for me. When Kelvin also disappeared I began to search the house myself and discovered them both in a bedroom I had never seen before with Hilary, a blonde whose beauty was marred only by eyes that looked in opposite directions.

On one occasion, rather than make the long walk home, we slept over. The walls of the bedroom were unplastered and a wooden 'chandelier' with candles hung from the ceiling. Five of us tried to squeeze into bed but eventually Oliver was dispatched to sleep on the chaise longue. Ian insisted I lie on my side next to the wall and somehow he managed to lie on his back. He wouldn't allow me to sleep next to John because he didn't want us to touch and neither would he turn his back on John. I lay and watched the water running down the stone wall – it was a very long night. The next morning John leapt out of bed first, smeared his face with Oil of Ulay, and made coffee to warm us up. His pugs, Oscar and Bertie, were released from the kitchen and we sat shivering, the coals of the fire long dead and the revels of the party a pleasant memory.

The atmosphere was very 'Noel Coward' – there was a certain pride in its elitism. One evening a couple of Macclesfield yobs were barred entry. When they asked why, John replied, 'Because you're disgusting!' At times it was insisted that the guests all wore hats or a particular type of clothing. The boys posed in the Macclesfield Arms wearing tailcoats, aloof and disinterested in the rest of the customers. All those dashing and handsome young men and most of them eyeing each other!

John Talbot regarded Ian as being quite ordinary, which he was in comparison to some of the eccentrics in the antiques world. Ian exercised a quiet enjoyment of these friendships and nobody seemed to mind when they realized he wasn't gay. While Ian did wear make-up, it was fashionable at the time and he didn't stand out as being overly flamboyant in his dress and manner. To John Talbot it was Ian's strong personality that projected itself and it was clear that nobody influenced him apart from his idols. Oliver Cleaver's parents forbade him to visit John at the shop – in John's opinion, missing the point that Ian Curtis had a much greater effect on their son. At the same time, Ian's parents had begun to blame Ian's lifestyle on Oliver.

It was well known that, after music, Ian's second love was his clothes. He yearned to be noticed and he accentuated his imposing image whenever he could and with little difficulty. Shortly before Christmas 1973, Ian set eyes on a tiger-print scarf in the window of a men's clothes shop in Macclesfield. He knew he wouldn't have any spare cash until it was almost Christmas and so he kept going back to the window to check that the scarf was still there. I went in one day and bought it as a surprise Christmas present. My pleasure was spoiled because of the distress it caused Ian when he thought Oliver had been in the shop and beaten him to it!

People who knew Ian from that time remember him for his gentleness and thoughtful sincerity. Possessions never really meant a great deal to him and, although his passion lay with buying records, once the shine had worn off he would be amenable to lending or giving them away. He was generous to a fault and it seemed to give him much pleasure.

John Talbot said of Ian's death: 'I was confused because everything I read about him made him out to be a doom merchant and I don't remember him like that. Music does propagate myths and people have tried to make that myth more than it was.'

CHAPTER TWO

Walk with me
Tube Hold & See.

Ian's family moved away from Macclesfield in the late spring of 1973 when Ian was half-way through his first A level year. Ian had had enough of the King's School and probably it had had enough of him. Once he decided to quit, there was no reason for the family to remain in Macclesfield, so they bought a house in New Moston, Manchester, from a friend of Aunty Nell. Ian's intention was to continue studying for his History and Divinity A levels at St John's College in the city centre, but after only two weeks he began to argue with his tutors and stopped attending lectures. He told me that he couldn't agree with the views of his new tutors in the same way that he could with those at the King's School. For a while he felt unable to tell his parents what had happened and spent two evenings a week walking the streets.

   In the summer of 1973 I took a holiday job at Parkside Psychiatric Hospital in Macclesfield. I was interested in training to be an occupational therapist and thought that working there for a few weeks would give me a good insight into the job. I had already worked there the previous summer, but since then there had been a staff change. The atmosphere was more oppressive than I remembered and the painful inertia of the patients was typified by an old lady called Eva. It had taken her a full twelve months to progress from peeing on the floor at the department entrance to sitting down and making a small teddy bear. Perhaps my depressing tales of the mental hospital spurred Ian on, but he began to think seriously about moving to London. When Jonathan King announced he was looking for talent, Ian went down to the big city and queued with the rest of the hopefuls. He took nothing with him; he had no demo tape, not even a lyric sheet, yet he expected Jonathan King to recognize his obvious talent!

Ian saw an advert in a newspaper asking for young men to apply for jobs abroad. Again the interview was in London and Ian went down to find out what it was all about. The job turned out to be the position of gigolo in the South of France and Ian was asked if he would be willing to entertain rich old ladies. They photographed him while he talked. I don't know whether he was offered the post, but he was allowed to bring home some of the pictures.

After I took my O levels, Ian set about persuading me to follow him and leave school altogether. He implied that he had no real wish to date a schoolgirl and, to be fair, it took little persuasion for me to leave. All my close friends were leaving and I was nervous about making new ones, so I gladly took the easy way out. The idea of studying elsewhere appealed to me and I was keen to start again in an establishment where I felt I could be more anonymous. I disliked drawing attention to myself and in retrospect I think that was one of my main assets for Ian. I was there as an accessory, with little danger of ever outshining him! I enjoyed the attention I thought he was giving me, genuinely believing that he knew best. I stopped wearing make-up because he said I looked better without it and tried not to displease him by going anywhere without him. 'We'll get married,' he said. 'Don't worry about a job. I'm going to make so much money you'll never need to work.'

I passed seven O levels and looked at the local college of further education, intending to take my A levels there, but Ian seemed distressed at the idea of me having even more opportunity to mix with men. He balked when he realized that I wore a short skirt rather than jeans to look around the college and insisted that should I enrol at the college, I would not wear make-up. His anger frightened me, but I pushed it to the back of my mind. I told myself that he would change when he felt more secure in our relationship. Indeed, it was hard to reconcile Ian's attitude towards me when other men were around and his attitude when we were alone. He liked to take me on long, rambling country walks. The solitude and the silence seemed to make him happy and he was never more charming and loving than on these occasions.

I'm not sure Ian himself knew why he would suddenly become so angry. He seemed to have a great deal of hate inside that was always directed at those closest to him. In the autumn of 1973 we went to a Lou Reed concert at the Empire Theatre, Liverpool. My parents kindly offered to drive us there and visit relatives while we went to the gig. We had to leave Macclesfield quite early, so when they picked me up from my photography class at college, Ian was in the car. The familiar pout and glower were already in place. When he surreptitiously showed me the quarter-bottle of gin in his pocket, I realized that he was well on his way to oblivion.

Immediately on entering the theatre, he began to drag me around by the hand as if searching for something. The last place he pulled me into was a vast, white, bright room full of men, who turned around and shouted at me. I couldn't believe that Ian had actually taken me into the gent's toilet, but he decided that it was all my fault and turned on me. I still didn't understand why he had drunk so much in the first place, but I knew I wasn't going to enjoy the performance. By the time we found our seats I was crying, my head ached with the tension and I began to feel nauseous. A man in the row behind could hear Ian's seething remonstrations and offered me some painkillers. Ian tried to prevent me from accepting, but I took them anyway and had to suck the pills because I couldn't swallow.

I had a Saturday job in a lingerie shop in Macclesfield and in the evening I would take the train to Manchester and meet Ian at Rare Records in Manchester city centre. The Rare Records job was incredibly important to Ian. He swotted for the interview by reading all his back copies of the music press and was thrilled when he was offered the job in the pop department in the basement. Ian allowed me to use the train to Manchester because he wanted me to be there as soon as possible, but he insisted that I make the journey home on the bus because it was cheaper. It was also twice as long and very cold.

Yet in some ways Ian could be very soft hearted. He was always hungry and forever buying greasy food from dirty-looking street traders. One balmy evening we were walking through Albert Square in Manchester. There were hyacinths in the window boxes of the town hall and the scent was overpowering. Ian took one bite out of his hot beef pie before spotting a lone tramp huddled on one of the benches. Barely able to chew the piece in his mouth, he went over and handed the pie to the tramp.

After only three months of my A level course, Ian asked me to look for a job and start saving for our marriage. Already bored with study, I accepted a clerical post in quality control at ICI pharmaceuticals. During the week we spoke to each other every night on the phone. Sometimes he would hint that he might have taken another girl out, or that he was seeing someone else, but any attempt to make me jealous was foiled by the fact that I trusted him implicitly. Also, because of his overwhelming jealousy, I assumed that two-timing me would be the last thing he would do. Moving to Manchester had brought about a change in Ian – as far as I knew he had stopped experimenting with drugs. This was a great relief to me because I (mistakenly) assumed he was happy. As someone who had never so much as smoked a cigarette, I found his desire for escapism through drug-induced detachment incomprehensible.

Ian's bedroom was the front parlour at his parents' house and it was here we sat, hour upon hour, listening to Lou Reed and Iggy Pop. I didn't mind this as I had developed my own favourites. The only album of Ian's that I never took to was Lou Reed's *Berlin*. One afternoon he decided to read to me from the works of Oscar Wilde. He chose 'The Happy Prince'. It tells the tale of a bejewelled statue and his friendship with a swallow. The bird postpones flying south for the winter in order to help the sad prince. The swallow picks off the jewels and gives them to the people of the city who are suffering. 'Dear little Swallow,' said the Prince, 'you tell me of marvellous things, but more marvellous than anything is the suffering of men and of women. There is no Mystery so great as Misery. Fly over my city, little Swallow, and tell me what you see there.' As Ian's voice neared the end of the story, it began to crack like the leaden heart of the statue and he cried like a baby.

A constant obstruction to the potential smooth-running of my life, Ian made it difficult for me to feel comfortable in my first job. His persistent questioning about the men I worked with would make me self-conscious about becoming friendly with anyone. He would telephone every night and interrogate me. We argued during one such telephone conversation and Ian deliberately put his foot through a glass door at his parents' house.

He was my first lover but one evening his unfounded, obscene ranting and raving about my friendships with previous boyfriends got out of hand and I became ill. My father took time off work the next day to take me out to lunch. He and my mother hoped it was an end to my relationship with Ian Curtis. They had always found Ian strange, although up until then he had behaved towards them in a fairly innocuous manner. Initially, it had been the earring, the sunglasses worn in the dark and the Marlboro smoke that bothered them. What alarmed them later were his selfishness and his desire to be the centre of attention. Ian turned up in Macclesfield the following Friday. Knowing that my mother wouldn't allow him over the threshold, he booked in at the George Hotel on Jordangate.

As we sat in Sparrow Park that night, I endeavoured to let Ian down gently. I suggested we stop seeing each other for a while or just not see so much of each other. He was distraught and kept on and on, begging me to reconsider. Eventually I gave in and agreed to carry on with the relationship, promising myself at the same time to try to finish it another day. The next morning, armed with a bouquet for my mother, he apologized to her. She did her utmost to feign forgiveness, but I knew she was still furious.

On 14 February 1974, Ian gave me another valentine card with a rhyme inside. It described a dream he'd had about me, walking alone and lonely on a deserted beach – definitely not a love poem. I threw the card away as I felt that he was trying to frighten me. Nevertheless, the dream was to come true in June 1980 in Carnoustie, Scotland, where I holidayed with my parents and Natalie after Ian's death.

Despite my earlier resolutions, Ian and I became inextricably tied and I couldn't or wouldn't imagine my life without him. He never forgot that I had tried to end our relationship. As a warning, he told me that I had no choice but to marry him since no one would want what was irretrievably 'his'.

We got engaged on 17 April 1974. The engagement ring held half a dozen small sapphires surrounding a minute diamond and cost £17.50 from Ratners. What impressed me most of all was that Ian sold his guitar to pay for it. My parents had offered me either an engagement party for all of our large family, or an eighteenth birthday party for my friends the following December. Ian chose that we should have an engagement party. It didn't seem to matter to him that owing to sheer numbers we would not be able to invite our friends. He was fond of telling me that his friends didn't really like me, so it didn't matter to me either. He also pointed out that an engagement party would mean presents for our future together, but an eighteenth birthday party would mean presents for me personally. His views seemed practical and the way he put it made it sound as if he only wanted the best for our married life. By the time he had finished, I felt selfish for even considering a birthday party. The only friend I invited was a close one from school, Christine Ridgeway. He had outlawed all my other friends.

My Liverpudlian family came to Macclesfield in its entirety. If anyone knows how to party, they do. No one had any intention of driving home, so there was no need to worry about how much anyone was drinking. They gathered in the kitchen and told raucous jokes, they danced in the dining room, and they chatted in the lounge. Meanwhile, Ian's family sat perched uncomfortably on the edge of the settee. They didn't drink alcohol but wanted endless cups of tea, which kept my mother tied to the kitchen.

As I downed a few drinks I began to get into the swing. While I was having a quick dance with one of my younger uncles, I didn't notice Ian glowering at me through the doorway. When I joined him in the hall, he took hold of his Bloody Mary and threw it upwards

25

into my face, covering it and my dress in thick tomato juice. Christine tried to referee between us. There was no need because my main concern was that no one else should know what he had done. In fact I covered up for him. His family left shortly after I reappeared in a new outfit. My mother guessed what had happened, but I denied it.

Ian did try to join in with the fun, but he danced alone rather than with me. His stiff, contorted movements and static, staring pout assured him of a large if puzzled audience. As my relations looked at each other bemused, I experienced a strange mixture of embarrassment and glee at his individuality. The next tantrum came when Ian realized that we would not be able to have a room to ourselves for the night. In a three-bedroomed bungalow with dozens of guests looking for somewhere to put their heads, it wasn't surprising. The next day, despite the not altogether innocent parties at the antique shop, Ian gave me a lecture on the excesses of drink and how various aunts should have conducted themselves. My grandmother went home convinced that Ian was 'on drugs'. I only wish he had been; at least it would have provided me with an excuse for his behaviour. Even then, my mother voiced her fears about Ian's split personality, but I was horrified that she could suggest such a thing. My relationship with Ian had almost become an act of defiance.

We did have a small engagement celebration with Kelvin Briggs and Elayne King when we went to Jilly's in Manchester for a Bowie/Roxy Music night. Whether it was to save money or for devilment, I don't know, but we took our own drinks hidden inside our coats and didn't buy a round all evening. I was sorry that Helen and Oliver weren't invited and got the impression Ian thought getting engaged was 'uncool'. Ian lived his life by a conflicting code that changed depending on who was there at the time and what he could gain from it.

Ian left his relatively secure job at Rare Records and hired a stall on Butter Lane antique market, round the corner from the record shop. This was an obvious bad move. I don't think he ever made enough money to cover the rent. Initially all the stock came from Ian's per-

sonal record collection. He bought new stock only once and the pro-
prietors of the market complained that Ian's goods were not strictly
antique. I had taken a job at Macclesfield Borough Council and was
working in an office next door to an auctioneers'. One lunch hour I
bought a job lot of 78 r.p.m. discs, hoping that they would satisfy
Ian's critics. I don't know if Ian actually sold any records while he had
the stall. His collection diminished, but he never made any money.
Even his prized copy of Bowie's *The Man Who Sold the World*, with the
cover picturing David Bowie wearing a dress, was allowed to go.
Jubilantly, he told me he had sold it to a young boy, but it transpires
that he had given it to Helen Atkinson Wood. He had managed to
keep in touch with some of his old friends, despite forbidding me to
see mine – including a male penfriend I'd had since I was thirteen.

Eventually, Ian could no longer pay for his seat on the indoor market and began looking for a job. He applied to the Civil Service and
was given a post at the Ministry of Defence in Cheadle Hulme. Just
before he took up the post, he spent a day in Manchester with Aunty
Nell. She helped him to sort out his wardrobe for his new job and he
had his hair cut in a smarter, more spiky style. They had their photographs taken in a photo booth and they both looked so happy. Ian
laughed when he told me later that Aunty Nell was pleased about his
new job, but warned him that there might be homosexuals in the
Civil Service. After a few months with the Ministry of Defence, he
was offered another job working for the Manpower Services
Commission in Sunley Building, Piccadilly Gardens, Manchester,
which was much nearer home.

We spent almost every weekend at Ian's parents' house. This occasionally annoyed his father but he lost his temper only once and even
then nothing was said to me directly. Ian liked to take me to the gay
pubs and clubs around Manchester, especially the Rembrandt,
Napoleon's and the Union. There was an old transvestite at the
Union who called himself 'Mother' and sang bawdy songs. It embarrassed me that we behaved in such a voyeuristic manner, but I was
embarrassed even more when one night we bumped into a couple of
friends from Macclesfield. When the flustered 'Hellos' were over, we

embarked upon a gay pub crawl. Our friends introduced us to some of the regulars and Ian was able to talk to them for a long time. He had an intense interest in the way other people lived, especially those who led lives which were out of the ordinary. I didn't want to know about the poor unfortunate man who was beaten up in the toilets on Park Green in Macclesfield.

Other times we would go to the Bier Keller on Saturday nights and get legless before catching the last bus home. Ian's mum and dad would wait up for us. I would sleep in Ian's bed and he would sleep on the living-room settee. At bedtime, Ian always insisted on going to the bathroom first. He was still obsessed with his complexion. He wore antiseptic cream most of the time like thick make-up, adding an extra layer when he went to bed. His friends and mine thought it rather funny, but he never went anywhere without checking his skin.

Ian liked to laugh with his parents and he pulled his mum's leg all the time. He would say something utterly ridiculous while just out of earshot and she would pop her head out of the kitchen with a look of disbelief, to see Ian sliding down into the chair in a silent, quivering laugh. His jokes were always teasing, but never spiteful.

In 1974, when we attended the wedding of my cousin Susan in Liverpool, the occasion was marred when Ian forbade me to dance, as he considered the scooped neckline on my cotton dress to be too low cut. I judged that even Ian would not dare to make a fool of himself in such a public place, so I danced anyway and ignored Ian's sullen, miserable face. I thought it unreasonable for him to try to spoil my fun again. Luckily he was restrained, but insisted we make love on the train home to Manchester. By now I was used not only to Ian's jealous and possessive attitude, but also his particular brand of retribution. I felt he was re-establishing ownership.

CHAPTER THREE

Face to Face

Once we had named the day, our wedding preparations seemed to set themselves in motion. Ian showed little concern for the arrangements, but knowing his fetish for making sure my body was covered I chose a high-necked wedding dress. He didn't like other men to look at me. I also bowed to his request that one of the hymns would be 'Glorious Things Of Thee Are Spoken', sung to the music of Haydn which is the same tune as the German National Anthem. Although I enjoy the flamboyance of the church, I hold the cynical view that some of the Christians I know are the most 'un-Christian' people. In fact, initially Ian was reluctant to marry me in a church. He predicted I would be struck down as I walked along the aisle.

On the eve of our wedding, my insides were churning and my own and my mother's nerves were in shreds. As I ironed my going-away dress and counted my 'sexy knickers', I felt afraid rather than excited. I convinced myself that the feeling that things 'weren't right' was just wedding nerves, but I still had an understandable desire to take more than a few steps backwards in time. Since then I have discovered that Ian had doubts of his own. He told Lindsay Reade (Tony Wilson's first wife) that he had thought about cancelling the wedding because he knew in his heart that he would eventually be unfaithful.

We were married on 23 August 1975 at St Thomas's church, Henbury, followed by a reception at the Bull's Head in Macclesfield market place. Ian chose Kelvin Briggs as his best man, which surprised me as I thought Oliver Cleaver was a closer friend. However, his choice was a good one as Kelvin was more dependable and responsible. Ian wore a peach-coloured pinstripe suit from Jonathan Silver in Manchester and looks terribly dated in the photographs. He worried himself silly about how he would look in a suit. He had visions of Oliver outshining him by turning up in black leather, which I suspect was what Ian would have preferred to wear. The event seems to have had little meaning to Ian or his friends. Oliver told me that he was surprised when Ian got married and commented, 'The wedding was almost secondary to what we were all going to wear on the day.'

Despite all this, everything went according to plan. Ian looks very handsome in our wedding pictures and his face is full of expectant pleasure – a mien which would gradually be lost. Young and stubborn, we were determined to prove people wrong. We were out to put the people who predicted an early divorce firmly in their place.

We spent our wedding night at the Lime Tree Hotel near Victoria Station in London. It took so long to wind our way to the top of the building, I was beginning to think it was some kind of joke but, yes, this tiny room was ours for the night. As Ian sank into contented sleep, I lay awake listening to the traffic. In the morning I pounced on Ian, nearly piercing his bare foot with my stiletto heel. His anguish released my apprehensive tension and, gratefully, I sat down on the bed and sobbed at last.

We stayed at the Hotel Pretty on rue Amelie and the honeymoon was planned with Ian's usual zealotry – no ordinary visit to Paris. The Crazy Horse rather than the Moulin Rouge, the Modern Art Museum not the Louvre, and so on. He must have scoured every arty magazine to find unusual places to go and yet he missed out Père Lachaise cemetery, where one of his heroes, Jim Morrison, is buried.

One evening he took me to a mysterious club. On paying to get in we were handed some minute pieces of plastic fruit and led along the corridor to a blue room full of enormous cushions. We sat there alone for about fifteen minutes, totally devoid of ideas as to what would happen next. Eventually a man took away the fruit and returned our money. Looking back I realize we were probably expected to make love. I suspect Ian thought he would be watching rather than participating.

The rustic Parisian tavern we visited looked extremely inviting. It was called 'Au Lapin Agile', ('jumping rabbit') but we paid a small fortune to get in. Once inside, we positioned ourselves around a wooden table. So did the rest of the customers, to my surprise. Ian ordered our drinks and then quite unexpectedly, everyone else around our table burst into song. Not conversant with French folk songs I didn't know whether to mime or slide under the table, but Ian insisted we sit there and listen to the lot.

On our return from Paris the purchase of our house had still not been completed. We had searched all of Macclesfield for a house we could afford. At the time there were many on the market that needed renovation. Most were the traditional three-storey weavers' cottages. The top floor was a garret room with a very large window to give the weavers plenty of light. The cottages were riddled with woodworm and had no bathroom. Eventually, Ian's family found a house in Chadderton. This was on the outskirts of Oldham and a short bus ride from Ian's parents' house. We still had to borrow £100 from Aunty Nell, but house prices were much more reasonable in that area. Until our completion, we lived for a short time with Ian's grandparents in the Manchester suburb of Hulme.

Ian had always had an interest in reggae music; Bob Marley and Toots and the Maytals already figured in his diverse record collection. Moving into that area of Manchester gave Ian the opportunity to throw himself into the local culture. He began to spend much of his time in a record shop in Moss Side shopping centre, listening to different reggae bands – although, as our cheap record player was packed away ready to move to the new house, he spent very little money there . Once again Ian became obsessed with a lifestyle different from his own. He began to infiltrate the places where white people didn't usually go. He took me to the Mayflower in Belle Vue, which at best was a seedy version of the Cotton Club and at worst a place where they held tawdry wrestling matches.

The Britons' Protection, in the Knott Mill area, was also a regular haunt. That particular spit-and-sawdust establishment did not serve women – I was thrown out. Rather than take me somewhere else, Ian stood with me in a dingy corridor which ran alongside the bar. It seems that women were allowed to imbibe in this tight spot. The main reason for our visit was that we were waiting for the club next door to open. The Afrique Club was a small, dark place up steep, narrow stairs, not far from where the Haçienda now stands. The tiny dance floor was empty and a few black people stood around the makeshift bar drinking from bottles. The eye-opener was that they were not served from behind the bar, but from a crate on the floor in front of it. I felt like an invader and very conspicuous, so I was glad to get away.

It was clear that we still had a lot to learn about each other. The next time Ian took me there with Kelvin Briggs and his girlfriend Elayne. The club was busier, the crate had disappeared and our drinks came with glasses. As we stood around, the disco started playing George McCrae's 'Rock Me Baby'. A girl stepped on to the dance floor and began to take off her clothes. I squirmed with embarrassment. After a few seconds I was furious with Ian for taking us there and I marched out. Kelvin and Elayne followed me, but Ian stayed put. When he eventually came out, we had a screaming match in the street. He was very angry with me and accused me of objecting to the stripper because she was white and most of the men watching her were black. I explained to him that I simply objected to having to watch a stripper, full stop, but he said I'd changed since our wedding.

The parties in Macclesfield petered out. Oliver Cleaver and Peter Reid went to Oxford, John Talbot moved down to London, as did Helen Atkinson Wood, who had a place at Goldsmiths College.

It was extremely tedious for us, as a young married couple, to share a home with Ian's grandparents and at times they must have felt equally uncomfortable. For me, the main problem was trying to study for A level English Literature on day-release and, naturally, I needed to read. For the sake of privacy, their curtains were never opened more than an inch or two and Ian's grandfather would not allow me to have the light on during the day. Living like a mole made it very difficult to study and, as winter approached, we huddled together in the same room every evening to keep warm.

However, Ian felt at home there. Even when we had signed the contract to our own house, he continued to find reasons why we could not move in, but I was keen to set up my home as a new wife. The atmosphere at Stamford Street, Hulme, became stifling – only pride prevented me from packing my bags and going 'home to mum'. Ian's grandparents treated us too well, running around catering for our every need. I found myself being cosseted to the point of insult and felt less independent than when I had lived with my parents. There were two round-pin electricity sockets in the entire house. This meant that, among other things, we could not have a washing-machine. To my embarrassment Ian's grandmother wanted to hand wash all our clothes herself in the kitchen sink. We weren't allowed to contribute towards our keep – not a single penny. Although Ian seemed not to care, I felt ill at ease with the imposition we were making. All our feelings towards each other became stifled – from holding back on our love-making to keeping a lid on our disagreements. One evening we went up to our room to argue in privacy. Ian's grandmother came into the bedroom and sat between us on the bed. One way of getting out of the house was to walk the streets of Hulme collecting money for the pools coupons that Ian's granddad usually sent off.

Eventually, we made the transition to Sylvan Street, Chadderton. Ian was determined to turn it into the home he had imagined, but it was hard to realize his dreams on a civil servant's salary. He had extreme ideas about decor – for instance, he didn't want us to have any wardrobes. After using suitcases for a while, he conceded and let me have an old single wardrobe which I had used as a child. It was painted white to blend in with the walls. Rather than have a carpet or rugs in the bedroom, the floorboards were painted gloss black and our bedspread had to be black and white with only a hint of grey. Later, on a return visit to Butter Lane market, we bought a pine chest of drawers – with black handles, of course. Ian knew he would not be able to write without a room of his own and logically he chose the second bedroom. I pointed out that he would not be able to play his

33

music in there as it was next to the baby's bedroom in the adjoining terrace. Undeterred, he painted the walls of the room what was supposed to be blood red. He painted and painted, the walls soaked up the paint and remained a deep pink.

The bathroom was on the second floor. One night, I was in a giggly mood. I waited until Ian went to the bathroom and hid in the red room at the bottom of the stairs. When Ian passed the door, I leaped out and gave a loud cry. I was stunned when he scurried on all fours to a corner of the landing and cowered there, whimpering. Seconds later he was up on his feet again. He descended the rest of the stairs as if nothing had happened and resumed his television viewing. I wanted to ask him about the incident, but I could tell that he was completely oblivious to what had happened. I sat and watched him for a while and soon even I was scarcely able to believe what I had seen. I pushed it to the back of my mind once the moment had passed.

Although Ian did speak about applying for jobs in London once or twice, he had abandoned his plans to leave the North. I didn't want to move to London and all I had to do was to point out the difficulties of selling our house and finding somewhere else to live. This was always enough to put him off making a move, as he knew he wasn't capable of focusing his mind on it without my support.

Starting a new life in Oldham wasn't easy. We had no friends there and the pubs in Oldham had a peculiar atmosphere. When we walked through the door all eyes were upon us. It was obvious to the rest of the customers that we were not Oldham-born and the bar staff were reluctant to serve newcomers. Our existence had become boring and the fact that we both hated our jobs didn't help. While Ian contented himself by continually 'nipping out for sandwiches', I became very depressed. Sometimes I was unable to stifle the tears on the long bus journey home. We had mistakenly saddled ourselves with a mortgage and a stability we weren't ready for. We were still only nineteen years old and Ian's ideas of a musical career didn't seem like extravagant dreams at all. They gave us something to look forward to; a way out of the hole we had dug for ourselves.

Practicality was not one of Ian's strong points, so I took on the role of 'carer'. I looked after the finances and as long as Ian had his cigarettes he may as well have been living with his parents. The main drawback about Ian's attitude was his inability to say 'no' to anyone. People knocking on the door to con or coax money out of us were invariably invited in. Ian would sit and listen to their spiel and was incapable of telling them we didn't want or could not afford their goods.

Ian told the Liberal candidate in a local council election that we would both be voting for him. On the day of election the poor man appeared at the door with his car to take us to the polling station. Ian accepted the lift and voted Conservative as he always would do. He argued that as his wife I had to vote the same way, otherwise I would cancel his vote!

It didn't take long to realize that married life was not going to be as comfortable as we had expected. We had very little spare cash for socializing and trying to keep the heating bills to a minimum meant that only the living room was warm. There were storage heaters in the house, but Ian refused to use them; in fact he disconnected one of them and lugged it into the back yard. The only thing he didn't economize on were cigarettes. As a non-smoker, I was exasperated.

Ian found it difficult to continue with his writing because there was nowhere he could find a comfortable solitude. The restrictions of living with relatives were lifted and our relationship would have been stormy if not for Ian's refusal to communicate with me. This was one way in which he would avoid confrontation. One night he turned his back on me in bed once too often. I bit into his back in desperation. Shocked by the faint tinge of blood in my mouth, I was rewarded by being kicked on to the floor.

CHAPTER FOUR

WHERE FANTASY ENDS

Once our home life had settled into a routine, Ian became frustrated with his lack of involvement in the music business. Tony Wilson had already presented *What's On* on Granada TV, and it was clear that something was beginning to bubble right under our noses. Unknown to me, Ian placed an advertisement in the music press in the hope of getting a band together. He signed himself 'Rusty' and had only one reply. This came from a guitarist called Iain Gray. He was a gentle figure, who enjoyed cracking jokes and for most of the time managed to cover up the fact that he was still grieving for his mother who had recently died. Ian began to see him on a regular basis, initially to exchange ideas about song writing. The two of them began searching Manchester night-spots and pubs for others to join the band, and met Peter Hook, Bernard Sumner and Terry Mason in the process.

As if being summoned to a religious gathering, we all assembled at the Lesser Free Trade Hall, Manchester, on 20 July 1976 to see the Sex Pistols. Ian had missed them the first time, much to his dismay. This was their second gig at this venue. He strode along looking for the right building and as I ran to keep up with him, he hurriedly explained that this band 'fought on stage'. There weren't as many people there as history would claim, but everyone who was to become anyone attended.

Peter Hook, Bernard Sumner and Terry Mason were sitting somewhere in front of us and although Ian spoke to them, he did not introduce me. Four small waifs strutted across the stage dressed like cronies of Oliver Twist. I wondered who was the mastermind behind this plan, but Ian was ecstatic. Seeing the Sex Pistols was confirmation that there was something out there for him other than a career in the Civil Service. Their musical ability was dubious that night, which reaffirmed Ian's belief that anyone could become a rock star. After the performance everyone seemed to move quickly towards the door. It seemed as if we had all been issued with instructions and now we were set to embark on a mission.

Ian's determination gathered momentum. In August of the same year we packed one borrowed rucksack and hitch-hiked to Mont de Marsan for the punk rock festival. For me it was a welcome opportunity to go on holiday. For Ian it was business – part of his career strategy. A bus and a boat-train took us to Paris. As we sat in the square at Saint-Cloud and devoured the last of our packed sandwiches, we didn't suspect it would take us at least two hours just to get out of Paris. Once on the N10, it was comforting to know we were at least on the right route, but I can't imagine why anyone ever picks up hitch-hikers. Every time we got into a car with a couple, they invariably had a row. One person would want to take us as far as possible and their partner would want to eject us at the earliest opportunity. Then there were the two German hitch-hikers who insisted we walk behind them. We bowed to their superiority and allowed them to pass us. They were picked up within minutes. I'm afraid to say that at one time we were so desperate for a lift that Ian hid in the doorway of a tobacconist's and left me alone at the side of the road. When a businessman in a smart car stopped, Ian ran out just in time to jump in.

After yet again causing an argument between a French couple, we were dropped on the outskirts of Bordeaux. There wasn't another vehicle in sight and by the time we trudged into the city I was beginning to panic. We didn't have a tent, it was nearing closing time for the hostel and, worst of all, Ian's allergy to the sun had begun to take effect. Ian had always told me that he was allergic to the sun, but I had never seen it before. His hands were crimson and had swelled to resemble a huge pair of red rubber gloves. The busy port reminded me of Liverpool and I had visions of us perched on a park bench all night, afraid to go to sleep. Ian was very calm. He simply approached a young man buying petrol and asked him for a lift to the hostel.

Panic over. They bandaged Ian's hands, although they seemed scep-
tical of our story that the sun was responsible. When two boys who
were sharing Ian's dormitory came to bed, he closed his eyes and stifled his giggles as they discussed his bandaged hands lying motionless on top of the covers.

The following night was spent in Captieux. There were two hotels,
one on either side of the road, so we chose the cheaper looking one. After
battling with the language and the uncooperative waitress, we managed
to be served with one omelette and a plate of peas between us.

Despite all this we did reach Mont de Marsan. The festival was
held in the stone bull ring, where we sat and consumed the cheapest
wine ever trod while our skin blistered and curled before our eyes.
The bill included Eddie and the Hot Rods, Roogalator, Pink Fairies,
Nick Lowe, the Tyla Gang and the Gorillas. The most memorable
band to play there, and in fact the only band I do remember, was the
Damned. I thought Ian would try to talk to them, but he hardly
moved never mind spoke to anyone. During the afternoon, several
people collapsed from heat exhaustion. In the evening, the music
stopped when a violent thunderstorm caused the open-air stage to
become electrically unsafe.

We tried to sleep that night, first on the concrete seats in the bull
ring and then on the wooden park benches outside. At dawn we
began our way home, but there are many routes out of Mont de
Marsan. Even after the early morning mist had lifted, we could not
decide which was the correct one. A man and his small daughter
eventually gave us a lift to Arcachon and a welcome bag of tomatoes.

Arcachon is a town with wide white-sand beaches, pine trees, fresh
seafood and a silent, heavy heat. The youth hostel was full and, as we
did not have a tent, we took the ferry across to Cap-Ferret intending
to hitch to Bordeaux from there. As we sped along in the alarmingly
small boat, Ian dragged his sore hands in the sea water.

The journey back to Paris was a good deal quicker than the journey
to Mont de Marsan and after having our last thirty francs conned out
of us in the Gare du Nord, we were glad to be back on English soil.

When Ian took me to see Iggy Pop in Manchester early in 1977, he introduced me to Peter Hook and Terry Mason who were sitting directly in front of us. As Hooky and Terry grinned at me from across the seats, I decided that this was more like it. Their enthusiasm and energy was boiling over and at last Ian had made contact with some realistic candidates for 'the band'. 'Where's Barney?' asked Ian. Pete made a movement with his hand, indicating that Bernard was under the thumb. That was the best gig I had ever been to. The audience were ripe for intoxication and Iggy Pop – the original punk – did not disappoint us. Most of us clambered up to stand on the back of our seats, save Ian who was too tall. There were too many of us for the bouncers to prevent it. As I stood swaying and rocking, I held on to Ian's head to balance, not caring if the seat collapsed – the music was all that mattered. Throughout, Ian was surprisingly still, despite David Bowie making an appearance on keyboards. Perhaps he hoped that it would soon be him up there on stage.

Our decision to move back to Macclesfield was made quite suddenly, but it was something I had wanted for a long time. We found Oldham very isolated and the arduous bus journey into Manchester every morning was depression itself. We were both working on flexitime and although it was Ian who insisted we start work as early as possible, he intensely disliked getting up in the morning. He held me responsible for easing him out of bed, but my efforts to get him to the bus stop on time were seldom appreciated. He would urge me to run on ahead in order to instruct the bus driver to wait for him. This I pretended to do every morning. By the time we arrived at Sunley Building, we would be arguing all the way up the escalators. I worked at the Department of the Environment in the same building as Ian, but on the sixteenth floor. It was my fault Ian had to get up in the mornings and it was my fault if he missed the bus. As soon as we met one of his work mates he would be all smiles, cheery and full of fun!

The Asian family we sold our home to were amenable and very polite, and even though they expected us to leave our meagre sticks of furniture behind, the sale went through smoothly. Ian could be very quiet and polite when it was required and it wasn't until I spoke to Pete Hook that I realized how racist Ian could be. Drinking spirits always had an adverse effect on his temper and it was only after one of these bouts that he began making vicious, prejudiced comments in an Indian restaurant. He talked about how one family took the toilet out of the house to make another bedroom, defaecated onto news-paper instead, and then threw it into their neighbour's garden. The rest of the band thought this outburst very funny, but this facet of Ian's personality was hidden from me and at the time I thought Ian shared my 'live and let live' views.

In the end the actual move was so badly co-ordinated that we had to move in with Ian's grandparents again. However, it would not be for too long this time. They would visit Ian's parents every Saturday and let us have the house to ourselves for the day. This gave me a chance to catch up on my hidden washing! Then I would stand in the back garden to put it through the mangle before hanging it on the clothes horse. It was a wooden affair which wound up to the ceiling on a small pulley. The whole ritual was reminiscent of my childhood in Liverpool and as I turned the mangle I couldn't help but think what a small distance I had travelled in such a long time. My life appeared to be almost pedalling backwards.

Ian's reggae fad had passed and he began to experiment with punk, but it was a half-hearted attempt. It wasn't in his nature to fol-low the crowd to an extent where he would not stand out. He bought a khaki jacket and wrote 'HATE' across the back in orange acrylic paint. This took a long time to dry and left an imprint on Kelvin's car seat. He would never have shown himself up by pogo-ing with the rest of them. When we went to gigs, I enjoyed being squashed and having to move in time to everyone else, but Ian was looking for a more individual way. He very much wanted to be the centre of attention.

Iain Gray had fallen into a routine of visiting us at the Hulme address every Saturday and although he had become literally part of the family, Ian's dream of having a band seemed to be displaced by the companionship he was providing for Iain.

While Ian was too soft-hearted to tell Iain this, he became fanatical about meeting the right people and going to the right places. I didn't object to staying late at city-centre clubs until the early hours, but Ian never let me sleep in and go to work late. We always had to be in work for 8 a.m., no matter how little sleep we had managed to get the night before. One night we were forced into catching a bus that didn't stop as close to home as we would have liked. We found ourselves crossing a deserted wasteland of rubble, streets with pavements and kerbs, but no houses. There was very little light and although I had no idea where we were, Ian didn't seem concerned and picked his way across in the gloom, with me hanging on to his arm in fright. Ever so quietly a car drew up alongside us. Ian pulled away from me and, leaning into the car, exchanged a few words before the driver cruised away. I asked Ian what had been said and he confirmed my worst fears: he had just been offered money for my services. I was furious with him for putting me in that position, but waited until we were in the safety of his grandmother's scullery before letting him know it. Ian said nothing. He turned around, brought two long hands up and put them around my neck, just tight enough to render me immobile. After a few moments, he released me and we went to bed. We were up and about as early as usual and the incident was never mentioned again.

Peter Hook, Bernard Sumner and Terry Mason had known each other throughout early childhood. When they all found themselves at Salford Grammar School, they joined forces and became great friends. As the punk era arrived, they began looking for a singer for their band. Numerous odd-balls answered Bernard and Terry's advertisement in Virgin Records, the most odd being a hippie who was dressed in what was clearly an old tasselled cushion cover. Danny Lee, a friend of Peter Hook, was said to be able to 'out-Billy Idol' Billy Idol, but he never actually managed to get up and sing. When Ian rang Bernard Sumner's number, Bernard remembered bumping into Ian at local gigs and made a snap recruitment decision. He told Ian there and then that he could be in the group.

'Because I knew he was all right to get on with and that's
what we based the whole group on. If we liked someone,
they were in.'

Bernard Sumner

This left Iain Gray very much on his own. He must have felt reject-
ed as he vented his bitter feelings on me at one of the last nights at the
Electric Circus gigs. His rude verbal abuse offended me, but as he
didn't touch me physically I didn't care. All I wanted was success for
Ian and, at the time, the number of casualties was unimportant. Also
Iain's attitude was a little unfair.

'Ian didn't want to let Iain down, so I think he waited until
Iain got fed up and left before he joined us. 'Cause Ian was
as soft as shit, wasn't he?'

Peter Hook

To determine whether Ian really could fit in with the rest of the
lads, Bernard arranged a 'getting to know him' session. This involved
an outing to Ashfield Valley near Rochdale. He found a soul-mate in
Terry Mason. They had both spent a large portion of their lives avid-
ly reading the music press and waiting in record shops, hoping to be
the first to buy each new release. They saw music as the main ingredient in life and believed everything the music press said. Ian in particular revelled in the tortured lives depicted in the songs of the
Velvet Underground; any music which didn't demonstrate a certain
sadness, violence, or perhaps a struggle against impossible odds, was
dismissed.

I decided to take driving lessons and even though Ian had no wish
to drive himself, he was very supportive. I enrolled at a school near
his parents' house so Ian could visit them while I was having my lesson. I had no car of my own and there was no one to take me for a
drive in between the one-hour lessons each week. One night my
instructor directed me to drive down a deserted back street in the
middle of Manchester and I found myself on a piece of wasteland
behind a derelict mill. Luckily the look on my face was enough to tell

him he had made a mistake. Not wanting to tell Ian what had happened, I carried on taking driving tuition from the same man until the day I failed my test. Ian was wonderful when he heard of my failure. I think at that time, if I'd committed murder he would have stood by me. His loyalty made him very stubborn and he was loath to admit that I didn't yet have the experience to pass the test.

The house in Barton Street, Macclesfield, was exactly what we had been searching for. It was double fronted and stood on a bend in the road. With a front door and staircase in the centre and a living room on either side, it was considerably larger than the neighbouring homes. The room on the left seemed as though it had been built to fit around the bend in the road and was almost triangular in shape. Eventually, this was to be Ian's song-writing room, just as he had always wanted.

The kitchen was compact and there wasn't a great deal of room in the shared yard for a washing line, so Mrs Moody had an old-fashioned clothes rack in the kitchen. It wound up to the ceiling on a little pulley, just like the one Ian's grandmother kept. As the Moodys would be taking it with them, Ian resolved to scrounge his grandparents' identical clothes rack for our own use.

On a snowy day in May 1977 we moved back to Macclesfield, or rather I did, as Ian was 'unable to get time off work'. By now I had become suspicious as to why Ian was never able to take leave, even though we hadn't been away on holiday that year, and he had always 'just nipped out' whenever I rang him at work. While living in Macclesfield, we carried on working in Manchester. Ian insisted we catch the early train each morning and start work at 8.30 a.m. in order to give us more time in the evenings. Ian seemed to spend his evenings meditating over a cigarette, while I sewed.

In the summer of 1977, Ian renewed his acquaintance with Richard Boon, manager of the Buzzcocks. He hoped Richard would show some kind of interest to help the band on their way, but when he suggested the name the Stiff Kittens, Ian was deeply irritated. This was most likely due to the fact that it sounded just like any other punk group. At last they settled on the name Warsaw, taken from

'Warsawa' on Bowie's *Low* album, which was less typical of the other names being thrown up for contemporary bands.

On Sunday 29 May 1977 Warsaw played their first gig at the Electric Circus. They were undaunted by the rest of the bill: the Buzzcocks, Penetration, John Cooper Clarke and John the Postman. Tony Tabac made an unrehearsed appearance as Warsaw's drummer. Tony had a very laid-back attitude, slightly upper crust and looking as if he would never have to earn one. It became obvious that he wouldn't quite fit in with the rest of the lads, but they persevered because they all liked him. Ian was disappointed by Ian Woods' review of the gig in *Sounds*. It picked on Bernard, saying he looked like an ex-public school boy.

Paul Morley was involved right from this very early start. He saw through the fact that they were still learning to play their instruments (and how to sing), but most importantly noticed that they were different. He wrote in *NME*: 'There's an elusive spark of dissimilarity from the newer bands that suggests that they've plenty to play around with … I liked them and will like them even more in six months' time.'

Once over the hurdle of that first gig, everyone took it for granted that there would be more. Warsaw started on the irritating and inevitable round of arguments with other bands about who was headlining, who was providing the PA, who was paying for it, and so on.

Around this time, Martin 'Zero' Hannett came on the scene. He was a student at Manchester University, and he and his girlfriend Susannah O'Hara began to promote local bands. They managed to find local venues in the most unlikely places, including an edifice nicknamed 'the Squat' on Devas Street, off Oxford Road. This was the worst venue – the surrounding landscape had already been flattened and the Squat stood lonely, waiting for its fate, yet bands flocked to play there. The first time I went there, I didn't believe anyone would be able to perform because I was convinced that the power wasn't even connected.

Warsaw considered themselves lucky to be on Martin and

Susannah's books and took to the dilapidated circuit with enthusiasm. The second gig followed quickly on 31 May at Rafters, a small bar beneath a larger club called Fagins in Manchester. Ian and I were already familiar with Fagins as he had taken me there to see the Troggs before we were married. During June 1977, Warsaw bounced backwards and forwards between the Squat and Rafters in Manchester. When Martin Hannett arranged one of the Rafters gigs, he had told Fast Breeder, who were managed by Alan Erasmus (an actor friend of Tony Wilson's), that they could go on last. Unfortunately he had made Warsaw the same promise. The two bands argued all afternoon. By 10 p.m., nobody had even had a sound-check. Fast Breeder went on first, as they realized people were beginning to drift home.

When Ian finally made the stage, he was so drunk and so mad that he smashed a beer glass and cut his leg, which at least made sure the remaining audience remembered him. As this was a midweek gig I stayed at home – one of us had to be sure of getting into work the next morning. That night Ian ripped his leather jeans to shreds, but I was able to stitch them and make them wearable. Despite the condition of the jeans, I assumed his legs would have been all right. In fact they were so badly cut he undressed in the dark that night so I wouldn't see. I suppose Ian's stage persona had already begun to get out of hand, but he obviously didn't want me to see him like that. The performances I saw were nowhere near as frenzied.

Ian was excited when they were offered the support gig with Johnny Thunders and the Heartbreakers at Rafters. That night was the first time Warsaw were ever called back for an encore and whatever they did after that, it never matched that specific feeling of elation and pride I had that night. From then on, gigs became more available and slightly further afield, including Eric's in Liverpool.

We prepared the triangular room of our new home for the composing of Ian's forthcoming masterpieces. He painted the walls sky blue, the carpet was blue, the three-seater settee was blue, as were the curtains. The only concession was the bright red spotlights and, later, a red telephone. He kept the old stereogramme in there too. Ian had no

45

craving for a hi-tech music system; it didn't seem to matter to him what he played his records on. We barely set foot in the streets of Macclesfield and as such our social life remained centred around Manchester.

Most nights Ian would go into the blue room and shut the door behind him to write, interrupted only by my cups of coffee handed in through the swirls of Marlboro smoke. I didn't mind the situation; we regarded it as a project, something that had to be done. Neither did I inspect his work. I never doubted that his songs would be anything but superior.

The majority of Macclesfield youngsters were still listening to heavy rock music. Rural life and fashion was at least ten years behind anything that might have been happening in Manchester. The atmosphere was that of intense anticipation, as if a huge tidal wave was on its way and everybody was determined to be on it. The Ranch Bar in Stevenson Square was a favourite meeting place. If you walked down Market Street, you would always encounter one of the Buzzcocks or the Worst. Everyone seemed to congregate around the city centre. They were afraid of losing the momentum; scared of missing out on an impromptu meeting. No one waited to have their talents recognized. Instead, they decided what they wanted to do and did it, be it pop photographer, producer, journalist, or musician. It was a deliberate snub of the London scene and, as far as music was concerned, Manchester was set to become the new capital.

Paul Morley was one of these hopefuls. To earn money he worked in a book shop in Stockport, but the love of his life was a fanzine called *Out There*, which concentrated on capturing the current exciting events happening around the area. Londoners finally realized that perhaps their city was no longer the centre of the Universe as they had previously thought, and Paul Morley found himself being asked to write about Manchester and its bands. He seized the opportunity and constructed a niche for himself. There was so much to write about, such a plethora of events, that he was able to push aside his initial shyness. Ian liked Paul Morley's approach and at home he talked about him as if he was the key to the band's anticipated success.

> 'We had the same interests and the same beliefs in the music and in what we wanted to do, the same dreams. The way I wrote about the group probably meant a lot to Ian. A lot of people thought it was indulgent and pretentious, but I meant it and I think Ian knew that. I always thought it was really funny because there was Ian up on stage singing intense songs and there was me writing about it intensely. And we wouldn't talk about it, but it was always in the shadows.'
>
> Paul Morley

In July 1977, the *New Musical Express* printed a two-page article entirely devoted to the Manchester scene. Written by Paul Morley, it put Manchester at the centre of what was happening in the music business and slated Londoners for their smug complacency. The main attraction in Manchester was Howard Devoto of the Buzzcocks and, later, Magazine. Together with manager Richard Boon he started the ball rolling, hence Ian's eagerness to get to know Richard Boon. A mishmash of personalities created the atmosphere of that epoch and each one was either photographed or mentioned in Paul Morley's writing, from the Drones (reputed at the time to be the only band in Manchester to have any money for equipment) to John the Postman (who would come on stage after every gig to sing 'Louie Louie'). Unfortunately, this would often lend the evening the atmosphere of a working men's club. Warsaw were described by Morley as 'easily digestible, doomed maybe to eternal support spots. Whether they will find a style of their own is questionable, but probably not important. Their instinctive energy often compensates for the occasional lameness of their songs, but they seem unaware of the audience when performing.'

Morley's observations about Warsaw were accurate. It was true many of the early Warsaw songs were a little lame. It was not until they had gained a small amount of recognition and publicity that they were able to begin to progress towards perfection. Had they taken the stage during the punk era to perform any of the classic tracks from *Closer*, they would have failed in their mission.

Scouring the music papers became an almost full-time occupation for Ian and they began to pile up in the bedroom. Suddenly it became very easy for anyone at all who had a band in the North to get a mention in the music press. Warsaw were an incomplete band. Drummers came and drummers went, each with their own particular problems. Terry Mason's attempts to learn to drum were unproductive and he was 'promoted' to manager; Tony Tabac was easy-going but outmoded and unreliable; then there was Steve Brotherdale. He was the drummer for the Panik who were being managed by Rob Gretton, DJ at Rafters disco, Manchester, and editor of the Slaughter and the Dogs fanzine. Steve seemed hyperactive – his eyes appeared to be everywhere but on the person he was talking to and he soon earned himself the nickname of Steve 'Big Mouth'. On 10 August 1977, he, his wife Gill and another member of the Panik came to my sister's eighteenth birthday party at the White Hart, armed with a chocolate cake laced with laxatives. They had the mistaken idea that it would be hilarious if the rest of the guests suffered from diarrhoea, but their main objective was to persuade Ian to leave Warsaw and join the Panik. We continued the discussion back at the house in Barton Street, but by then we had all over-indulged and were tired. It was obvious Steve had realized that there was no way Ian would make a move to any other band, but for a while he still kept hacking away.

Later that night I had my first taste of things to come when one of our neighbours took off her clothes and engaged Ian in a snogging session – not that Ian objected. It was just about daylight, so I flounced out of the house intending to walk to my parents' house. By the time I reached the Flowerpot at the junction with Park Lane and Oxford Road, Ian had caught up with me. He grabbed hold of my arm and tried to take me home while I held on to a nearby gatepost. The roads were deserted apart from one young lad walking in the opposite direction. He paused and looked at us for a while, as if he was contemplating helping me, but Ian screamed at him: 'It's OK, she's my wife!'

Although Steve Brotherdale was an excellent drummer, the power and aggression which initially got him into Warsaw became his downfall. The other members of the band found it impossible to work with such a personality. When he got out of the car to investigate a supposed flat tyre, they simply drove off and left him.

CHAPTER FIVE

SOMETHING MUST BREAK

As Warsaw became more popular they were offered more gigs, especially at Rafters, so there was an urgent need to find a good and permanent drummer. Ian placed an advertisement in Jones' Music Store in Macclesfield in what seemed an unlikely attempt at finding someone who would be worthy of the position. The only reply came from Steve Morris, a former King's School pupil who had been expelled while Ian was there. He very conveniently lived ten minutes walk away from us. He already knew of Warsaw after reading a gig review in the punk fanzine *Shytalk*. Steve was surprised to see an advertisement for what he thought was a punk band in a back-water town such as Macclesfield.

Barney, Hooky and Ian were delighted with him – like the missing piece of the Warsaw jigsaw he fitted in perfectly. Warsaw became a complete 'family'.

I was happy for Ian, too. Having a member of the band who lived nearby was advantageous for him and, moreover, it provided him with a companionship he had missed since losing touch with Tony Nuttall and Oliver Cleaver. We hadn't socialized in Macclesfield for some time, but now we were able to meet Steve and his girlfriend Stephanie and visit our old haunts.

Luckily for me, Ian used his knowledge of the Manpower Services Commission and the following September I began a TOPS course at the local college, learning shorthand and typing. Life began to improve during this time and we were very contented together. I was enjoying my college course and the Giro they gave me every week. Ian was still working for the Civil Service and he applied for a transfer from the Manpower Services Commission in Manchester to a job nearer home. There could not have been anywhere nearer than the position he was given – the Employment Exchange in Macclesfield. This was a real break as it enabled him literally to roll out of bed and straight to his desk only a hundred yards away on South Park Road. It was ideal for someone like Ian, who detested getting up in the morning. He found himself with a more responsible job which he thoroughly enjoyed. As Assistant Disablement Resettlement Officer, he worked closely with disabled people to ensure that they claimed the benefits to which they were entitled. He took an extremely personal interest in his clients and did his utmost to find employment for them. The job certainly highlighted the caring side of his personality.

Ian's mentor at that time was his superior, Ernest Beard. Although Ernest was a good deal older than Ian, they had quite a lot in common. Ian knew him as Ernie and spoke of him with affection and respect. They became good friends through the work they shared. Both were equally frustrated by the local firms that refused to employ disabled people and, later, Ian was to spend some time persuading Tony Wilson to spearhead a television campaign to help epileptics in particular.

The Department sent Ian on a course to learn about epilepsy. Once brought under control, this complex condition usually has no effect on a person's working life, but ancient prejudices are difficult to eradicate and employers are reluctant to take epileptics on in any capacity. Ian liked to talk about what he had learned and soon I felt as if I knew almost as much about the illness as he did.

On the weekend of 2 October 1977 the Electric Circus opened its doors for what was supposed to be the last time, but wasn't. The old cinema stood out on the flattened landscape. As we neared the building, Ian became visibly agitated. Even if only one band was going to play, it was going to be his. (In fact Ian didn't get his wish and Warsaw played on the Sunday night.)

Inside, the building smelled damp, and the polystyrene tiles at the back of the stage were rollered with black paint which gave the Circus 'ring' a homely, amateurish appearance. Warsaw's performance was rewarded with a place on the Virgin ten-inch album *Short Circuit* which comprised eight tracks, all recorded live over that final weekend. This was a dubious honour as Warsaw's name-change to Joy Division was imminent and the chosen track was not one of their best. Most people remember it purely for Ian's outburst about Rudolf Hess. However, the album captured the atmosphere of the time by including such diverse and intrinsically Mancunian bands as the Fall, the Drones, Steel Pulse, the Buzzcocks and Mancunian poet John Cooper Clarke. Paul Morley's dialogue on the inner sleeve eloquently sets the scene and by the time the needle hits the blue (if you were lucky) or black vinyl, you can almost smell the substances.

Although Ian was happy then, the other members of the band still regarded him as 'pretty mad' because of the peaks and troughs in his personality:

> 'It was this contrast of being nice and polite, and then totally manic when he was on stage. One night, during a performance at Rafters, he ripped the whole stage apart, pulling off these twelve-inch-square wooden tiles with nails in them and throwing them at the audience. Then he dropped a pint pot on the stage, it smashed and he rolled around in the broken glass, cutting a ten-inch gash in his thigh.'
>
> Peter Hook

Ian was often frustrated as he felt that fame for his band couldn't come fast enough. Bernard Sumner worked at Cosgrove Hall, who specialize in animation and TV commercials. He had started at the bottom and at the time was doing a great deal of tea-making. It was Ian's opinion that Bernard should break all barriers and pester every passing Granada TV executive until Warsaw were given a spot on someone's show. When this didn't happen, Ian called Bernard every name under the sun but only really showed his exasperation at home. Ian's belief in what he was doing was ferocious and he failed to understand Bernard's reasonable timidity. He remembers, 'I didn't even work for Granada in the first place. It was just an impractical bee in his bonnet about it. To be fair he was trying really hard to get us on television. He used to plague Tony Wilson and eventually he did do it.'

Ian persuaded our bank manager that we needed a loan to buy dining-room furniture, and so we were able to raise £400 towards the recording and pressing of what was to be the first Joy Division record – an EP called *An Ideal for Living*. The loan was taken from our joint bank account and the rest of the band paid us their share in instalments. I did raise a fleeting objection to sharing the financial responsibility of investing in the band, but after consideration, Ian's plan seemed the only way forward. He told me that his parents had refused to lend him the money and we had already borrowed from my parents to buy a new lounge carpet. T. J. Davidson owned the empty warehouse in Manchester where they and other bands, including Sad Café, rehearsed. An attempt was made to bring T. J. Davidson in on the deal to help with the finance, but he was reluctant to become their manager. Peter Hook believed that TJ neither liked nor understood the music.

Joy Division's debut release was recorded at Pennine Sound Studio, Oldham, in December 1977. Paul Morley offered to go with them as their producer, but fortunately (or not) a hangover prevented him from being in the right place at the right time! However, his relationship with them as part of the music press grew. He found them incredibly shy. At the first real interview they sat around a table for two hours barely uttering a word. Transcription of the interview proved difficult and so Morley pretended in his writing that Joy Division knew exactly what they were doing and held their silence as some kind of artistic statement. Joy Division's stage presence, the power they held, had nothing in common with the timid, giggling boys who would stand at the bar.

An Ideal for Living turned out to be very much an in-house project: Bernard designed the sleeve and Steve arranged the printing in Macclesfield. The sleeve was in fact a poster which, when folded into four, was just large enough to slide a seven-inch pressing between the pages. The poster itself depicted a member of the Hitler Youth Movement banging a drum, a German soldier pointing a gun at a small boy with his arms raised, and two photographs of the band members. In one of the photographs, Bernard manages to look like a member of the Hitler Youth himself, while Peter Hook with his boots and moustache resembles an off-duty squaddie. Within the details of the instruments, one vowel in each word is treated to an umlaut to complete the Germanic theme. We all met at Steve's parents' house to fold the posters and used plastic sandwich bags to stop the records falling out. The image on the sleeve fuelled more speculation about the name of the band and led to questions about Joy Division's political affiliations. However, the tracks quickly became outdated as Joy Division could barely keep up with their own speedy development. They had difficulty distributing the disc on their own and eventually sold them to Rabid Records.

The four lads probably played their last gig as Warsaw on New Year's Eve 1977 at the Swinging Apple in Liverpool. The club was the size of a back-to-back terraced house. By the time the band had set up, the venue had the atmosphere of a small youth club. At first the few people there stood politely in front of the stage, but when manners turned to disappointment, they all sat down on the floor with their backs against the wall. In desperation Warsaw launched into a cover of Iggy Pop's 'The Passenger' and the audience stood up again. The highlight of the evening was midnight – not just because it was New Year's Eve, but because in true Liverpudlian tradition everybody ran out into the street to welcome the New Year in. The Manchester lads seemed puzzled by the bonhomie.

The release of the EP in January marked the change of name from Warsaw to Joy Division after the disappointing news that there was already a London-based band called Warsaw Pakt. The essential ingredient for any band at that time was to have a supposedly shocking name. Names such as Slaughter and the Dogs and Ed Banger and the Nosebleeds were guaranteed to conjure up the image of a group who just might resemble the Sex Pistols. Most young hopefuls completely missed the sad fact that all they could ever be were pale imitations jumping on the inevitable band(!)-wagon. Ian told me that Joy Division was what the Nazis called female prisoners kept alive to be used as prostitutes for the German Army. I cringed. It was gruesome and tasteless and I hoped that the majority of people would not know what it meant. I wondered if the members of the band were intending to glorify the degradation of women. Telling myself that they had chosen it merely to gain attention, I gradually became accustomed to the provocative moniker and concentrated on the music.

Joy Division worked hard to produce a new, tighter image. The frantic punk-style songs disappeared and were replaced with strong melodies and lyrics worthy of closer inspection.

The band played their first gig as Joy Division on 25 January 1978 at Pips disco in Manchester. Tony Wilson had promised Steve Morris that he would come to see them, but he didn't make an appearance. They performed what seemed to me to be a very brief set to an audience which had at last latched on to Joy Division's special aura. I sat at the top of the steps above the dance floor and observed a fan as he ran across the front of the stage and quickly picked up a discarded set list written in Ian's giant scrawl. It amused me that someone wanted to collect the set list when the band had only been paid £60.

The balancing act between Ian's day job and gigging had begun. Ian went to the doctor because he had flu symptoms but came away with only painkillers. The following week he was so tired after playing until 2 a.m. that he tried to get a sick note in order to skive off. This time the doctor examined him and told him that he really was ill.

Living in Macclesfield again was almost as daunting as moving to a new town as most of our contemporaries had flown south. Sometimes if there was an antiques fair at the Drill Hall, we would browse around and perhaps meet up with John Talbot, who usually managed a stall. Kelvin Briggs was also still a very good friend, but we didn't have the fun we'd had when we were younger. Although Ian and I were happy together, it miffed me slightly that when the other girls at college held parties, Ian would never come.

One contact with the past came when Tony Nuttall called on us. This visit was marked by one of our neighbours calling the police because Ian and Tony had been seen walking over the roofs of the cars on Barton Street on their way back from the Chinese take-away. Apart from this, Tony and Ian had grown a long way apart, particularly in their politics. They were left and right wing respectively. Tony wasn't a passionate campaigner, but found that shared politics gave him an almost unconscious way of warming to people. His friendship with Ian had disappeared and he wondered if Ian also felt the gulf. For this reason, the conversation that day remained shallow as they sought some common ground. When Ian showed Tony Nuttall the *An Ideal for Living* sleeve, he was dismayed by the imagery and, listening to the music, found it wasn't really to his taste either. Their friendship never re-established itself.

I had bought my first car, a Morris Traveller, with a £160 tax rebate and passed my driving test in January 1978. Ian was pleased for me but it did nothing to encourage him to learn to drive, despite my nagging about how much he was missing by being a mere passenger. However, for me the car was an important symbol of my independence. Ian was happy to be driven around by Steve, but I revelled in being able to make my own decisions about which gigs I attended.

Unfortunately, I hadn't realized that Ian had no interest in learning anything practical at all. I had also assumed that just as I learned to cook as I went along, Ian would gradually pick up on the traditional male skills. Having a father who did everything for me, including heeling my shoes, gave me expectations that Ian simply could not live up to. Ian had always claimed to be ambidextrous – he told me that he had in fact been born left-handed and that his mother had forced him to write with his right hand when he was a child. But if this means he was equally capable with both hands then it would also mean he was equally incapable with both hands. Ian was often frustrated and embarrassed by his clumsiness.

As the musical rebellion against the power of the London labels grew, Ian's excitement was obvious. Of the Manchester Musicians' Collective Ian said,

'The Collective was a really good thing for Joy Division. It gave us somewhere to play, we met other musicians, talked, swapped ideas. Also it gave us a chance to experiment in front of people. We were allowed to take risks – the Collective isn't about music that needs to draw an audience.'

The reasons for Ian's absence from his Manchester job became apparent when I realized that more often than not he had taken time off to visit Derek Brandwood and his assistant, Northern Soul DJ, Richard Searling. They ran an RCA promotion department in Piccadilly Plaza, Manchester. Derek Brandwood had managed to acquire a display window in the ground-floor avenue which Ian and I passed every day, but apart from the display window, the office was unobtrusive and well hidden from the rest of the bustling city. It had become a meeting place for new talent in the city and, coinciden-tally, for Martin Hannett. It was Martin's suggestion that he and Derek work with Sad Café as a team and he told Derek that he would be able to get them a TV spot on Granada if Derek could arrange an interview with Iggy Pop for Tony Wilson. It was this that set the ball rolling as far as talent-scouting in the North-West was concerned.

RCA was the same record label that had signed most of Ian's heroes, including David Bowie, Iggy Pop and Lou Reed. Ian found it easy simply to walk into the office and have a chat with whoever was there. Ian wasn't shy about pushing himself forward where his musi-cal career was concerned and, having met Derek since, I can see how comfortable he would have made Ian feel. When Bernie Binnick of Swan Records was looking for a New Wave band from the UK to go into the American market, he contacted his friend John Anderson who just happened to run a Northern Soul label with Richard Searling. A classic case of being in the right place at the right time, Joy Division were chosen partly for convenience. They were still try-ing to sell the *An Ideal for Living* EP and were keen to begin another project. Ian took the initiative to set up a meeting between the band, Richard Searling and John Anderson. Peter Hook was the only mem-ber of the band to raise any real questions or to appear remotely wary. Joy Division were desperate to do some more recording and any queries Peter may have had were hastily pushed aside. Production or even the type of music they were to record was given little or no discussion. The only thing clear in their minds was the fact that someone else was going to pay for the recording.

Richard Searling, John Anderson and Bernie Binick agreed to put £500 each into the project, which was to be recorded at Greendow/Arrow Studios, Manchester, at £35 per hour. This was an expensive rate at the time, but it proved the serious intentions of the three investors. In April 1978 twelve songs were recorded: eleven composed by the band and 'Keep On Keepin' On' by N. F. Porter, which was reworked and the riff used on 'Interzone'. There are mixed views on these sessions. I remember Ian being very upset about the recording of his vocals. John Anderson had assumed the role of producer and Ian felt that whatever it was John wanted, he wasn't prepared to do it. He complained bitterly that he was expected to sing like a soul singer – James Brown in particular. A great deal of sulking went on when it was suggested they use a synthesizer, but the idea was taken on board.

The studio time wasn't all frustration and arguments. Some time was taken for the odd drink across the road and one night, when the band found their lagers devoid of lime, they changed the lyrics of 'Walked in Line' to 'We wanted lime'.

The album tracks themselves are a strange mixture, for at the time the band were experiencing a metamorphosis. Classic songs like 'Shadowplay' jostled for position against amateurish compositions like 'Novelty', which were written before each member of the band had discovered his own particular forte within the group's collective structure. Joy Division were unhappy with the recordings, realizing that they had moved on since beginning the project and had written new and more innovative songs. The three investors failed to recognize this and were disappointed with the band's lack of enthusiasm. The band were so desperate just to make a record that they had brushed aside their inexperience. Apart from the obvious complicated facets of the music industry, they had no knowledge of how to deal with businessmen. However, despite their displeasure with the work that had been done, the very fact that someone had paid for them to go into the studio appeared to kindle some interest from other sources.

Terry Mason was still struggling to book gigs for the band. Very often they played for free and on some occasions had to find the money to pay for use of the PA system. In the beginning Sue Barlow (Bernard's girlfriend) and I would stand at the front of the stage trying to look like an army of fans. Very much the pariahs of the Manchester scene, the band became downhearted. It seemed to them that the Fall only had to step out of the door to be offered a gig. Although Ian had spent a great deal of time trying to nurture his relationship with the Buzzcocks, the feeling among the band was that the only reason why Peter Shelley would stand next to Joy Division would be for protection if a fight was imminent.

> 'Most of the musicians in Manchester then were very middle class, very educated: like Howard Devoto. Barney and I were essentially working-class oiks. Ian came somewhere in the middle, but primarily we had a different attitude. We felt like outsiders: it was very vicious and back-biting.'
>
> Peter Hook

CHAPTER SIX

A NEWSREEL CLIP

When two London record labels, Stiff and Chiswick, decided to hold a 'battle of the bands' contest at Rafters, anyone who was hoping to be anyone joined a band, thinking they had a chance to be singled out by one of the record companies. Producers, managers, reporters, photographers – you name it, they were there, not in their usual roles but attempting to perform. In the clammy envelopment of the downstairs bar they jostled for a place on the bill.

Tony Wilson was already well known in the region after working on the local news programme *Granada Reports* and, later, having his own programme *So It Goes*. Every band Wilson had chosen to play on the show subsequently became famous. These included the Sex Pistols, the Clash, the Buzzcocks and Elvis Costello. Ian was most impressed when his long-time idol Iggy Pop was featured, so he had an understandable determination to get to know Tony. Tony had already seen the band as Warsaw on the last night of the Electric Circus and, despite the fact that he had enthusiastically waved the *An Ideal for Living* EP at the camera during his regional news programme, he had not yet been moved enough to get in touch.

As Tony Wilson walked down to the basement club to join that tiny elite, someone shouted to him, 'When's *So It Goes* coming back, T?' Before Tony had time to answer, another voice said, 'He doesn't want it to come back. He wants it to be gone for ever. Then everyone will remember it as a cult thing and it will become famous in retrospect.' Tony turned around and there was Rob Gretton. As Tony sat on one of the banquette seats near the pool table, Ian was a short distance away writing the most abusive letter he could muster. I was amazed that he thought he could get a TV spot by using such foul language. I blushed for him as he walked over and waited for the explosion when he had handed over the letter. Instead, he sat down next to Tony, obviously trying to summon the courage to speak to him. Being ill-mannered didn't come naturally to Ian, but he forced himself.

'You're a fucking cunt you are, you're a bastard.'

'Oh yeah,' said Tony. 'Why's that?'

''Cause you haven't put us on television.'

Tony reciprocated, not by giving Ian a return mouthful, but by telling him that Joy Division would be the next band he put on. Ian was elated that he had accomplished his mission. The next battle was actually getting Joy Division a place on the bill that night. When it became apparent that there would only be time for one more band to play, there was a ferocious argument between Joy Division and the Negatives, who included Richard Boon, Paul Morley and Kevin Cummins. Joy Division were justifiably indignant at the thought of missing their big chance because of what they considered to be a joke band and a scuffle broke out.

However, Joy Division got their way. At around 2.10 a.m. they took the stage and played three numbers before the plugs were pulled. The importance of the evening was magnified in the minds of the performers. If the whole show had been broadcast nationally, there could not have been more enthusiasm in that tiny club. Most people there were too naïve or inexperienced to know that groups who win competitions of this type disappear without trace. The event was significant – first, because of Ian's chat with Tony Wilson and second, because it gave Rob Gretton the opportunity to see Joy Division at their most determined and enthusiastic.

Tony Wilson remembered that he had already promised that they would be the next band he would put on screen. So when he had the opportunity for a 'What's On' spot during *Granada Reports*, he arranged for Joy Division to perform 'Shadowplay'. With monochrome footage of a dire cityscape taken from a *World In Action* documentary, the song came across as exciting and different. Joy Division would later be invited back to film 'Transmission' and 'She's Lost

Control'. Ian's verbal abuse had triumphed over the fervent competition that existed between the myriad bands spawned at the time.

Initially, the boys in Joy Division were greatly lacking in aggression. They all found it difficult to barter for the gigs which were in such short supply. While other bands found Joy Division to be aloof, arrogant and perhaps unnervingly sure of their eventual success, Joy Division covered their doubts well and thought other bands were more streetwise and ready for a fight. There appeared to be a social gulf between Joy Division and some of their contemporaries, and despite joining the Manchester Musicians' Collective, they didn't make many friends within the business.

One of their luckiest breaks came when Rob Gretton became their manager. A tough Wythenshawe boy, he was well equipped to guide them through the rigorous business of getting a deal.

> 'We all had a go at managing and we were all hopeless. It was too much to do and basically people don't like talking to musicians. They still think musicians are stupid. In fact, I'd agree with them on that; most of them are pretty stupid. I never got the feeling Ian was unhappy with Rob coming in.'
>
> Peter Hook

Ian made up his mind to accept Rob Gretton. After meeting him and his girlfriend, Lesley Gilbert, he told me how amiable they both were but repeated it almost to himself as if to reaffirm the decision he had either made or been forced into making. He spoke about them as if they were his guardians, or surrogate parents. Indeed, when the shit finally hit the fan it was to them we both turned. Unfortunately, Lesley and I would be at a disadvantage when later on Rob and Ian's relationship developed a confidentiality similar to that of solicitor and client, or doctor and patient. Ian had enjoyed organizing the deal with Derek Brandwood, but if he resented Rob Gretton taking over the situation, he never showed it. The most difficult thing for him to do must have been later when he gave up his job in the Civil Service and had to rely on Rob arranging regular monthly payments.

Ian was very lucky to fall in with such an easy-going bunch of people. They always accepted him the way he was. The white lies he told were taken simply as a part of him and never caused any major rows. Sometimes he would bitch about someone, but he would completely deny it when confronted. He hated it if anyone else went on holiday – not because he wanted to go away himself, but because he thought that time spent away was futile. He expected everyone to put all their time and effort into performing, as he did. Despite having more responsibilities at home than the others, he was much more dedicated and determined than they were. Once, when Bernard had taken yet another holiday, Ian put it to the rest of the lads that Bernard simply wasn't a good enough guitarist and that they needed a second rhythm guitarist to join the band and boost the sound. He even told me that they were auditioning in Bernard's absence. Bernard was furious when he found out and asked Rob Gretton whose idea it had been. Ian looked aghast. 'I never said that!' he said. It was this incident that brought Peter Hook's bass-playing more up front and made it a much more dominant part of their music. Later, it became one of Joy Division's best-loved trade marks.

Musicians' Union Collective meetings were usually held on Monday nights at the Band on the Wall. These performances were not so much gigs as rehearsals, accompanied by the jeering snipes of the Fall. Chaos usually reigned. One night we went out to buy chips and the bouncer would not allow us back in. On another occasion the rest of the band forgot to tell Ian that they were going on stage. He was in mid-pee when the sound of his intro (luckily 'No Love Lost' – a long one) filtered through the toilet walls. Reviewing one of the Band on the Wall appearances, a weary Mick Middles bemoaned Joy Division's 'limited' and 'samey' performance and suggested that the Nazi connection had been 'exploited beyond tolerance'. While in complete contrast Paul Morley, writing for the *New Musical Express*, described them as 'animated and volatile ...with eloquence and direction'.

Ian and I often met at home for lunch, but this was usually by coincidence rather than arrangement. One afternoon Ian was sitting waiting for me and told me that my parents had had to have my old dog, Tess, put to sleep. I was so inconsolable that I was unable to return to college. I felt stupid, crying like that over an animal, but being an animal lover too, Ian understood completely. Before the lunch hour was over, we decided that the only solution was to get another dog. When Ian finished work that evening we drove up into the hills to Windyway Kennels, the local animal sanctuary. A litter of chubby Border collies was just about ready to find new homes and we chose a friendly but frisky female. Ian named her Candy after the Velvet Underground song 'Candy Says' and was so delighted with her that I wondered why we hadn't thought of having a dog before. While I took it upon myself to housetrain Candy and teach her to sit, Ian readily volunteered for the walkies. He never made any attempt to persuade her to walk to heel. I can still see them together – a lanky young man being pulled along, arm outstretched, by a panting, over-excited dog.

The first night Candy stayed with us was unusually hot. We put newspaper down all over the lounge and left a small window open. Ian settled her down in a cardboard box with a hot-water bottle and hoped she would not be too lonely. During the night I awoke to hear her yapping. I waited to see if she stopped and when she did, I turned over and went back to sleep. The next morning I found the front door open and £7 – all the money I had – missing from my purse. This intrusion didn't worry Ian at all. He had nothing to say about it except that he was thrilled that Candy had guarded the house on her first night.

CHAPTER SEVEN

WALKING ON AIR

With hindsight, the decision to start a family was not a sensible one, especially as our finances were in such a precarious position. Nevertheless, hearing the other women at college talk about their children had made me broody. I tentatively began to talk about babies thinking Ian would probably suggest a more appropriate time to have one. Ian wasn't the type of man to discuss events logically and what he wanted most in the world was for people to be happy. If a baby would make me happy, we could have a baby. Ian insisted that there was no need to worry about money as by the time he or she was born, he would be making plenty. I wanted to believe him and my desire to start a family overcame any financial concerns.

When I did become pregnant Ian was pleased to tell his parents, but reluctant to tell the rest of the band. I was determined not to be the one that broke the news, but one night at the Band on the Wall, Bernard's girlfriend Sue said to me, 'You two are so close. I wouldn't be surprised if we heard the patter of tiny feet soon.' 'How did you know?' I replied. Ian looked so embarrassed, like a man who had made a blunder. Despite his apprehension, it was an anticlimax. Old-fashioned gentleman Hooky was concerned because earlier that evening he had allowed me to drive the transit van to the Greek take-away and now he didn't think it was appropriate in my condition! Yet I wanted everyone to know I was pregnant. Peter Hook was to say later that one of the problems with Joy Division was that they 'kept their relationships at arm's length and so did not share any happiness'. Already the very nature of my personality was at odds with band policy. It was almost as if it was unfashionable to be happy.

Ian and Bernard had become close. Ian enjoyed talking to Bernard about diverse, less mundane issues in life. Books, extreme concepts and philosophies all came under Ian's intense scrutiny. Institutions where people are locked away and forgotten about were one of his particular interests. My sister Jill had a friend who worked looking after the teeth of people in institutions and Ian loved to hear of patients with extra breasts along the nipple line. A simple harmless deformity would fire his imagination. Yet Bernard remembers that most of the time spent with Ian was humorous:

> 'The experience of being Joy Division was really, really funny and up, and the whole thing's been coloured by Ian. But we weren't a deep, heavy band, which no one will ever see. No records will show that; no films, videos, or anything will ever show that. We used to have a right laugh.'

In my view this humour was very private and detrimental to any other relationships each individual member of the band had.

On 28 October 1978 Ian and I were the witnesses for Bernard Sumner's marriage to Sue Barlow. Sue and I had become good friends. Being the original 'girlies', we had seen Joy Division develop from a schoolboy idea to the realization of a dream. They kept the wedding very low-key and so we were the only guests. Half an hour before the wedding I was driving Sue up and down Peel Green, Manchester, trying to find a florist so that she could have a last-minute bouquet. Afterwards we all trundled off in the Morris Traveller to the Last Drop Village in Bolton for a meal, which Bernard somehow managed to pay for with only £6 in his pocket! By this time I was irritated because he had made hurtful jibes about the speed of my beloved car and the main point of conversation over the meal had been the fact that he was not wearing any underpants. By contrast, Steve Morris arrived on our doorstep the following Saturday saying he wanted to take us both out for a meal. His only explanation was that he had £60 in his pocket and wanted to spend it all that night. I suppose the fact that I wrote to my sister and told her all this proves that I was already concerned about how we were going to cope when the time came for me to give up work.

Steve Morris became the first member of the band to change partners. A small group of female fans had begun to appear at gigs. With alarming regularity they would turn up before myself and the other girls and buy drinks for the band. Known collectively to us as 'the Goshes' because of the way they spoke, they were pleasant and very enthusiastic – possibly the first real Joy Division fans. Ian was especially keen that Steve should pair up with one of them – Gillian Gilbert. He would mutter through his teeth and sigh at their shy attempts to get to know one another and, in my ear, he urged Steve to make a move. Steve's long-standing girlfriend Stephanie was in for a painful separation.

Stephanie was a tall, eccentrically dressed girl, whose soft voice belied her stature. I hadn't got to know Steve and Stephanie very well, mainly because Ian had always insisted that Steve didn't want me in his car as there was only room for his 'friends'. So when tales of Stephanie's inability to accept the end of the relationship began to filter through via Ian, I took little notice.

One afternoon I came home to find Ian seemingly in a panic. 'Stephanie's in the bathroom,' he whispered. 'She's got razor blades in her handbag and she says she's going to kill herself.' Stephanie descended the stairs like a woman who was not intent on ending her life, but had merely visited our bathroom. I was surprised to see her, especially as she was acting as if she was an invited guest. Ian ushered me into the kitchen and urged me to leave by the back door and telephone Stephanie's father so that he could retrieve her. It wasn't easy to tell a man that his daughter had just threatened suicide, but I relayed Ian's story just as he had told me to. The three of us sat around drinking coffee and chatting. Stephanie still gave the impression that she had been invited to come and see us. She was perfectly at ease. There was no mention of suicide, razor blades or anything else unpleasant.

Some time later, Stephanie's father turned up in a taxi to take her away. She had no idea why we sent for him. She looked questioningly from Ian to myself and all I could say was that I was sorry. I remember the confused hurt in her eyes and Ian's refusal to discuss the event afterwards. For the rest of the day there was a look I interpreted as smug satisfaction on his face and I convinced myself that I had betrayed Stephanie. I could see no reason why Ian would cause such pain by setting Stephanie up and yet I felt as confused as Stephanie had looked. It crossed my mind briefly that he was in fact vetting Stephanie's suitability as a girlfriend of one of the band, just as he had vetted and dismissed my school friends. A comment made by Steve Morris when I interviewed him does little to clarify Ian's attitude towards Stephanie. He said, 'Sympathy was one of his qualities, particularly with regard to Stephanie. You can't be in a group without someone getting on your nerves – everyone did at some time.'

After coming into a small inheritance, Tony Wilson used his good fortune and financed the recording of the *A Factory Sample* EP. When asked to collaborate, Martin Hannett was able to realize his interest in Joy Division by producing two tracks for them: 'Digital' and 'Glass'. Peter Saville began to establish himself as Factory designer and chose the silver and black simplicity. Appearing to be encased in an extended sandwich bag, this double EP gave the public the opportunity of sampling what Factory Records would have to offer. Joy Division, the Durutti Column, John Dowie and Cabaret Voltaire each had room for at least two tracks, a sticker of their choice and a rectangle containing information about the individual recordings, which Joy Division left almost blank. Paul Morley said of their offering: 'How much longer before an aware label will commit themselves to this individual group?' Martin Hannett's production gave them a much cleaner and colder sound than had been previously heard on *An Ideal for Living* and which lacked the warmth and emotion he would later achieve on *Closer*.

One of the very few gigs I attended outside Manchester was the Check Inn, Altrincham, in November 1978. A young fan named Dean tried to persuade me that should we have a son, Dean was a nice name. His apparent shyness when asking Ian for his autograph was appropriate to a demigod rather than an up-and-coming young singer. Although it was exciting seeing the acceleration of Joy

Division's popularity, and I had believed in them from the beginning, there was a surreal quality as Ian's predictions and dreams began to come true.

Towards the end of 1978 my pregnancy became all too obvious and on 27 December Ian had his first recognizable epileptic fit. Joy Division were to play their London debut at the Hope and Anchor, but Bernard was in bed with flu. After some discussion it was decided that the gig had to come first, so Bernard was bundled into the back of the car wrapped up in a sleeping bag. As a first London gig the Hope and Anchor was a disappointment. Expecting the glamour of the capital city, Joy Division hadn't realized they would be playing in a pub cellar and that all the equipment would have to be lowered in through a trap-door. The small audience was not enough to spark the exhilaration needed to spur the band on.

Disappointment turned to turmoil on the way home. Bernard remembers that Ian's conversation about the gig had taken a rather negative turn and Ian had told me when he came home that there was even talk of him leaving the band. As Bernard tried to keep himself warm, Ian began to tug at his sleeping bag. A struggle followed and once Ian had the bag he wrapped it around his head so tight that Bernard couldn't wrestle it from him. Eventually, Ian's seizure surfaced and he lashed out, seeming to punch at the windows. Steve pulled over to the side of the road and when the fit was over they took him to the Luton and Dunstable Hospital.

I was dumb struck when Steve Morris and Gillian Gilbert finally brought Ian home. He had a letter for his doctor and some Phenobarbitone tablets. 'I've had some kind of fit,' he said, but I didn't really believe him. I thought someone must have made a mistake or perhaps he had faked it. All of us were astonished and unable to believe it. We took it for granted that the incident had been a one-off and that if there *was* any illness, it could be cured. I rang his office and mine and we both stayed at home the following day, expecting something else to happen. When I rang his parents they appeared stunned and unable to swallow the information I was giving them.

Ian's GP was disinterested. The most he could do was put Ian on

the waiting list to see a specialist. In the meantime, Ian was expected
to carry on with his life. His fits became quite frequent and frighten-
ingly violent. We tried to keep a record of how often and how serious
they were. It seemed extreme to go from having no fits at all to having three or four a week, and to become epileptic so soon after studying the illness was too much of a coincidence for me. I decided that it
must be something else and waited for them to diagnose it so that it
could be put right.

Ian never left the room without telling me where he was going
even if it was only to the bathroom and then he always left the door
unlocked. One evening he returned from walking Candy looking
badly shaken. The next morning the bruises on his back appeared so
severe that I thought he had been beaten rather than suffered a fit. I
went with him to the doctor again that morning, hoping Ian's injuries
would entitle him to more speedy treatment, but to no avail. Ernest
Beard came with us for that appointment. The doctor seemed mildly
amused when we all trooped into his surgery and after examining
Ian's back he merely shrugged his shoulders and sent us away to
wait for Ian's hospital appointment. Ernest Beard was a retired Navy
man who had worked on destroyers and had been involved in the
evacuation of Crete, and although he was experienced in working
with people who had all manner of problems, Ian did not really give
the appearance of needing his help.

> 'When Ian got epilepsy it didn't affect him, didn't stop him. I
> think he accepted his epilepsy. He was very happy-go-lucky.
> He had a great sense of humour. He would come in, in the
> morning, and it was obvious that he had travelled overnight
> from a gig. It never affected his work. I was amazed.'
>
> Ernest Beard

I knew Ian was quite knowledgeable about epilepsy and tried to
pump him for information. I wanted to help him but until he had
seen a specialist no one really wanted to use the word 'epilepsy'.
Ian's provisional driving licence arrived, but by now there was no
question of him using it. An epileptic can suffer from convulsions of

one or several types and for obvious reasons they are not allowed to drive. However, apart from this Ian had told me that once such a person had been prescribed the right anti-convulsant therapy, they would be able to lead a normal life. As the description 'normal' is somewhat ambiguous, it would have been easy for Ian to substitute it for 'boring'.

My parents began to worry about me and our unborn baby. As we couldn't afford to install a telephone, they paid for us to have one as this reduced the risk of my being isolated in an emergency. Ian registered himself as disabled. He told me benefit claims are processed as a matter of urgency for disabled people.

While Ian was busy rearranging his personal life, the band were becoming more and more in demand. On 13 January 1979 Ian appeared on the front cover of *NME* sporting the soon-to-be-famous long green raincoat and the inevitable cigarette. This honour was down to Paul Morley's persistence. Morley's earlier attempt at getting Ian that particular spot had been thwarted when the editor insisted on using Joe Jackson instead. At the end of the month the first John Peel session was recorded. Joy Division had definitely arrived and although they had worked so hard for so long, it all seemed sudden and bizarre. Sandwiched in between these two important landmarks in the band's career was the realization that Ian's illness was something we would have to learn to accommodate.

It was 23 January 1979 before Ian saw a specialist at Macclesfield District and General Hospital. He arranged for various investigations to be carried out into Ian's condition and prescribed Phenytoin Sodium and Phenobarbitone. Phenytoin Sodium is a long-term treatment most commonly used to treat epilepsy. Its side effects include slurred speech, dizziness, confusion and gum overgrowth. Phenobarbitone is an anti-convulsant used in combination with other drugs and its side effects are drowsiness, clumsiness, dizziness, excitement and confusion. I am sure Ian was warned of all these side effects and he did tell me that he would need to see the dentist more often to keep a check on his gums. The possibility of confusion was also mentioned. I thought, 'Hell, what's a bit of confusion if it stops the fits?' I

71

felt that Ian was safer now because he was in the hands of the hospital, but at the same time there was a certain finality, an impotent acceptance.

We realized that there was no turning back the page – Ian was now EPILEPTIC. He was open about it at first, but that soon ceased. I thought he had begun to settle into a new, more careful way of life, but in fact he became withdrawn, moody, and reluctant to discuss anything except the most mundane and necessary. He appeared to resent my cheerfulness, my willingness to carry on, but I was determined to keep our lives on an even keel. It was Ian who may have joined the British Epilepsy Association, but I had to read the newsletters and magazines. They were crammed full of advice on how to lead a normal life, including case histories, how to look after epileptic children, details of outings and holidays, and advice on the problems of epileptics themselves – how to deal with other people's attitudes, how to get a job, etc. There was almost everything you needed to know, yet there was no mention of the problems epileptics could cause within the family. There was no talk of depression or other behavioural difficulties with adult sufferers.

Bernard Sumner had been aware of Ian's manic personality; his moods would fluctuate between ultra-politeness and blind rage. Now that Ian was taking medication for his illness, these mood swings seemed more extreme. One minute he was high and the next, he wanted to cry. It crossed Bernard's mind that the tablets were making him more unhappy than the epilepsy itself.

> 'I think there was something a bit special about Ian. I know people say that, but I really do mean it. I can't stop saying this ... I really do think it was the tablets that killed him. I really do. I know it.'
>
> Bernard Sumner

As my pregnancy continued, I found that I wasn't able to get enough rest. I had to wait up for Ian even later than before. After a gig he would not go to sleep until he'd had a fit, and it became a ritual for him to sit there and wait for an attack. He was afraid to go to bed in case he died in his sleep, as (so he told me) one of his clients who was epileptic had choked in her sleep. Very often he would go into an absence seizure, where he would be motionless and seemingly unaware of his surroundings. I would watch him perched on the edge of his seat with a lighted Marlboro still hanging between his lips. Because he was so much taller than me, I felt rather helpless. For those few minutes, I could only make sure he didn't hurt himself. We would both lie in bed at night and listen to his breathing, waiting for the change in pace that would signal an attack. It was as if these fits were an insurance against having one while he was asleep.

Ian told me of the band's decision to change its name if one member 'left'. I thought this was a strange thing to have discussed and wondered if they were expecting something to happen to him, or whether they were planning to throw him out.

Although he was very well liked by staff and customers at the Job Centre, Ian still had to work full time and this caused problems if he needed to leave Macclesfield early. Not all Ian's colleagues were sympathetic to his dilemma. Once, when Joy Division had to play a gig during the week, Rob Gretton arranged for Tony Wilson to pick Ian up at the Job Centre. Tony left Granada Studios in Manchester to collect Ian at exactly four o'clock, as that was the earliest they would allow him to leave. They drove down to London, not knowing precisely where the gig was. They decided to ask a queue of young people if they knew the way, only to find that the queue was for them! It made the hassle at work worthwhile, but Ernest Beard was worried about Ian. He found the reviews in the music press disturbing. In his opinion they were like psychiatric reports, even using the appropriate terminology and references. Journalists and fans seemed to have picked up on Ian's instability all too soon. Ernest himself left work early one day so that he would be able to see Joy Division on *Granada Reports*. He said he thought the presentation was terrific, but asked Ian if he had taken any drugs to help him. Ian replied that all he had needed was a 'Gold Label'. Indeed Ernest remembers, 'He was always laughing and joking. When I was in the business, they used to say that an overdose was like a common cold. They see such a lot of it.'

Certainly Ian's dancing had become a distressing parody of his off-stage seizures. His arms would flail around, winding an invisible bobbin, and the wooden jerking of his legs was an accurate impression of the involuntary movements he would make. Only the seething and shaking of his head was omitted. This could have been a deliberate imitation, but his dancing was not dissimilar to the way he had danced at our engagement party four years previously.

> 'The first time anyone saw him do it there were only about four people there, so he had the entire floor. He leapt off the stage and was doing it all over the place. I thought it was cracking. I didn't get any feedback that anyone thought it was comical, because it was obviously so intense. One or two people did things like that around that time in that city and you might have thought he was a bit ... but he just seemed like he was on the edge. He was scared.'
>
> Paul Morley

The lyrics Ian chose to match the band's already haunting music were increasingly depressive and if you wanted to believe that he was writing about someone else's experience, then you also had to believe that he was capable of enormous empathy. Journalists and fans alike tried to decipher his words and now, of course, many feel that Ian's melancholy was staring them in the face. It was too incredible to comprehend that he would use such a public method to cry for help. Peter Hook was consistently described as surly and defensive about the meaning of the lyrics. He never considered Ian's lyrics to be more than a part of Joy Division's work and definitely not the guiding force it was purported to be. In fact Pete didn't take any notice of Ian's lyrics until after his death; only then did he recognize that Ian was (in Pete's words) 'a real beautiful wordsmith'.

Ian carried a plastic bag around which was full of notebooks and paper on which he wrote frantically when the mood took him. He would listen to the music, which was more often than not arranged by Bernard, and choose lyrics that seemed appropriate. If the lyrics worked well with the melody and gave the listener something of depth to think about, then there was no reason to question Ian's means. Undoubtedly, Joy Division's audience wanted more.

In an interview in the fanzine *Printed Noises*, Ian said, 'We haven't got a message really; the lyrics are open to interpretation. They're multi-dimensional. You can read into them whatever you like. Obviously they're important to the band.' Ian himself had always enjoyed reading into other people's lyrics. We used to argue about the last line of Lou Reed's 'Perfect Day'. I thought the words were 'You're going to reap just what you sow', but Ian's interpretation was 'You're going to read just what you saw'. One of his ambitions was to witness events as they happened, before reading about them in the press.

> 'He fooled around more than anybody. He would do anything for a bet. He made writing songs a lot easier. He had a lot of words in his book. He would just sit there with his book and not move very much, mumbling something and getting a few bits of paper out. We didn't have quality gear and wouldn't quite know what he was singing, but just the fact that someone had got some words and got something to sing meant that we could write songs very easily.'
>
> Steve Morris

> 'He was a catalyst for the rest of us. He would … cement our ideas together. We would write all the music, but Ian would direct us. He'd say, "I like that bit of guitar, I like that bass line, I like that drum riff." And then I would arrange it – mostly I would arrange it, with additional suggestions from the other members of the band. He'd put the lyrics in later, but he always had some ready. He had a big box with lyrics in. He brought our ideas together in his own way, really. That was the first thing we missed … He came up with all the vocal melodies … He did some guitar on one or two, but it was pretty straightforward. He hated playing anyway. We made him play. He played in quite a bizarre way and that to us was interesting, because no one else would play like Ian. He played in a very manic way. We thought it was good; we liked the way he did it.'
>
> Bernard Sumner

Between 24 January and 13 March 1979 Ian had several more *grand mal* attacks. During these, his body would twist violently and I would worry in case he bit his tongue or banged his head. He had attended Macclesfield Hospital for an electroencephalogram (EEG), where metal tags are glued to the scalp to record the electrical activity of the brain. His medical records state that no abnormalities were found. Presumably no one was any closer to finding out what was causing Ian's illness.

Gradually, his prescription was changed to try to bring the attacks under control. Each time Ian collected his new tablets he was full of renewed enthusiasm, convinced that this time the formulation would help him. Over the following months he took Carbamazepine, Phenobarbitone, Phenytoin and Valproate. Carbamazepine reduces the likelihood of convulsions caused by abnormal nerve signals in the brain. It has less of a sedative effect than similar drugs, unless mixed with alcohol. I lost track of which tablets he was meant to be taking and which ones he had finished with.

There was so much happening in the Spring of 1979. It seemed that everything we had planned was finally coming to fruition, from the birth of our child to Joy Division's first album. Rob Gretton was keen to tie up any loose ends and eradicate anything that might jeopardize the band's future. The recording for the RCA subsidiary had long since been finished when Rob Gretton became the band's manager, and Richard Searling raised no objection to his involvement as he felt the band needed someone who really understood what they were trying to do. The first thing Rob Gretton did was to suggest a complete remix.

> 'Because RCA had shown quite a bit of interest, we didn't feel that we wanted to do a remix. We felt that RCA would pick it up as it was and any remixes that needed doing would be done by RCA from their budget. But the guys were very determined. I'm sure they were right that they didn't want to go with a major. They didn't want to be seen as another Sweet, or Bonnie Tyler, or whatever.'
>
> Richard Searling

The album was outmoded and under-produced and although Joy Division were quite right to request a complete remix, it would not have sufficed and there was not an infinite amount of cash available. They had reached a stage where they desperately needed Martin Hannett's diverse ideas before they could go any further. So much time had elapsed since the initial recording that Joy Division were no longer the same band. In the ensuing inertia Richard Searling had lost control of the project and despite RCA's obvious interest, a year after the recording was made it was decided to abandon the project altogether.

One Monday evening in January, Joy Division, Rob Gretton, John Anderson, Richard Searling, his wife Judith and I met in the Portland Bars beneath the Piccadilly Hotel. The master tapes were handed over in return for £1,500 – the same amount of money that had been spent on the project originally. The publishing contract had never been signed, leaving the band free to re-record the songs if they wished and retain the publishing rights for themselves. The subsequent bootlegs appear to have been taken from a cassette copy and not from the original master, as has been previously suggested.

Unknown Pleasures was recorded in April 1979 at Strawberry Studios in Stockport. This and the initial pressing of 10,000 copies were paid for by Tony Wilson. To say Ian was impressed by Martin Hannett's work would be an understatement. He came home enthusing about the sampling of glass-smashing and hand-clapping. Hannett already had considerable experience recording unusual sounds and atmospheres, and his marvellous production of Joy Division's drums became an integral part of the music. His ability to translate their thoughts and needs into a co-ordinated work of art was the catalyst Joy Division badly needed. Ian appeared to be happy with his new playmates, and I did everything I could to help him organize his life and reduce any stress he might be under.

Whether it was intentional or not, the wives and girlfriends had gradually been banished from all but the most local of gigs and a curious male bonding had taken place. The boys seemed to derive their fun from each other. Ian intensely disliked foam rubber and hated touching it, and when Joy Division could at last afford flight cases, they amused themselves by pulling bits of foam from the insides and dropping them down the back of Ian's neck. Nevertheless, he managed to overcome this fear when he had to help Candy out of trouble. One afternoon I arrived home from a hospital check-up to find the lounge ankle-deep in foam rubber. Heavily pregnant, I had walked all the way there and back and was exhausted – seeing what Candy had done to the settee made me want to cry. Ian got down on his hands and knees, picked up every scrap and restuffed all the cushions. Then he went out and bought me a box of chocolates – this was typical behaviour from the Ian I married.

When things began to go well for Ian and his band, he thought of his old friend Tony Nuttall and decided to include him in the excitement. He wrote to Tony and invited him to design a sleeve for the album. Unfortunately Tony was in the final year of his degree and was unable to take up his offer. I was surprised to learn that Ian had been in touch with him as he never mentioned it.

I confess I showed little interest in the recording of *Unknown Pleasures*. My main concern was that Rob Gretton didn't book any gigs for the week the baby was due as I desperately wanted Ian to be at the birth. Ian was amenable to this. In October we attended talks at the ante-natal clinic and he never appeared remotely squeamish about the prospect. While some husbands were visibly panicked by the graphic video we were shown, Ian had an embarrassing fit of giggles.

As the 6 April came and went my doctor decided that the birth should be induced on 16 April, which was Easter Monday. The evening before, Ian and I sat watching a documentary about the Nuremberg trials when he suddenly turned to me and said, 'I can't imagine there being another person here with us.' I thought to myself indignantly that he wouldn't have to imagine for much longer! I went upstairs and climbed the stairs to our room. As I plonked down on the bed, my waters broke.

Ian bundled me into an ambulance that night, but didn't come to the hospital until the next day when the birth was imminent. I was the complete coward. I drew the line at an epidural, but took everything else they offered me. I screamed and swore and was so frightened I felt I would have done anything to keep the baby in. When it was all over, Ian said that if anything had gone wrong it would have been my fault as I had 'done it all wrong'. I like to think that he wasn't prepared for the strength of his feelings on seeing his own child's birth. Ian's initial fears turned to joy and the trauma was soon forgotten.

Natalie was tiny; my father said he had seen bigger chickens. Her features and hands were like Ian's in miniature. Everyone could tell she was our first child because we both spent every visiting time gazing into her face. Ian was completely enraptured. In those days new mothers were encouraged to stay in hospital for longer and everything seemed to be going well, until the afternoon when I told Ian we would both be coming home the following day. Suddenly Ian seemed extremely apprehensive and dismayed. He said nothing and I carried on talking, pretending not to notice his change of attitude.

When I tried to ring him to ask him to come and collect us the next morning, there was no answer and he hadn't gone to work. My mother and her friend had no trouble getting into the house as Ian had left the front door unbolted. He'd had a fit and cut his head during the evening.

Natalie and I soon settled into a routine, but Ian was terrified something might happen to the baby. He was reluctant to hold her in case he had a fit and dropped her, and so could not bring himself to participate in looking after her as much as he might have done. I begged him to try to hold her for a short time alone, but he had convinced himself that it would endanger Natalie if he supported her unsupervised. Ian's fits were never totally unexpected and shortly before each attack he would experience what is usually described as an aura. I pointed out to him that he could easily put the baby down if he had any such warnings, but he said he did not want to take the risk. I accepted what he said – after all, Ian knew more about it than I did.

Instead I had to look after the both of them single-handedly. At times this was both infuriating and tiring. Ian expected his evening meal to be ready when he came home from work and if Natalie was crying he would not even hold her while I dished out the food. To some extent I felt he was demanding his turn for attention from me, like a jealous child.

CHAPTER EIGHT

ON A RAZORS EDGE

By May 1979, Joy Division were used to playing at the Russell Club in Hulme, Manchester. Tony Wilson hired what was in effect a social club for tenants of the council flats and once or twice a week its name was changed to the Factory. It was a bleak place, mirroring the area in which Ian had lived during his adolescence in Macclesfield. Hundreds of dark windows stared at the car park outside the club and I was forever haunted by the feeling that I was being watched. Of the many Factory gigs, this one was particularly important for me – it was my first evening out since having Natalie.

Ian and I drove there together and after I had parked the car we walked across to the doors of the club. I was still half a stone overweight, but managed to squeeze into a pair of jeans. Ian put his arms around me, kissed me and said how proud he was of me. To him, I looked the same as before. It was a great set. The band were better than ever and they had built up a serious following. I stood in the audience admiring my husband with everyone else. I considered myself to be well organized in my new role. I felt self-satisfied and happy in my ignorance – I believed the depressive image and emotive lyrics merely to be part of the act. Joy Division were on the brink of success and despite other people's misgivings, I was holding on to my husband and my baby. Even before Natalie's birth, Mr Pape, my old boss at the County Court in Macclesfield, had warned me that I may not be able to have both.

It would be wrong to say my personality didn't change when I became a mother. My life was no longer centred on Ian. Now I had this small person who was totally dependent on me. I had always felt responsible for Ian's well-being, but when our daughter arrived I naturally expected him to adjust and make her the centre of his life too. Not that I stopped caring for Ian, but Natalie always came first and in refusing to help me I often felt that Ian was pressurizing me to choose between them. My mother would give me little hints such as, 'Before he comes home from work, move the drying nappies away from the fire to make him feel welcome.'

Joy Division were gigging regularly during May – at least one a week, sometimes two – and were even interviewed on Radio Manchester. It was hard for Ian as he was still working full time, and his doctor had advised him to get early nights and not to work too hard. On the evening of 24 May 1979 we were having a quiet night at home. He began to feel unwell and had four *grand mal* attacks, one after the other. I was unable to wake him from the fourth attack, so I rang my mother to come and look after Natalie and then called an ambulance. He regained consciousness in casualty and was kept in hospital for a few days.

It was purely common sense that prompted me to call an ambulance and it appears I knew less about epilepsy than I thought. I read in a book, which wasn't published until 1984, '*Grand mal status epilepticus*, in which the subject does not recover consciousness between generalized tonic-clonic convulsions, is a medical emergency.' Following this, a brain scan was arranged at Manchester Royal Infirmary. This could have shown up cysts, scars and abnormal blood vessels in the brain, or even have identified a tumour – but the results were normal.

Ian did not have any epileptic attacks during June 1979 and he did try hard to settle down into the relative tranquillity of family life. We lived a very short distance from South Park in Macclesfield and on warm summer evenings we would take Natalie in her pram and walk the dog. For me at least, these times were idyllic.

In July, Mick Middles reviewed a Factory gig for *Sounds* and obviously saw something in Joy Division's music which he had not previously noticed. After calling them 'orgasmic and mind-blowing', he went on to say:

'During the set's many "peaks" Ian Curtis often loses control. He'll suddenly jerk sideways and, head in hands, he'll transform into a twitching, epileptic-type mass of flesh and bone. Suddenly he'll recover. The guitars will fade away, leaving the lonely drummer to finish the song on his own. Then, with no introduction, the whole feeling will begin again. Another song, another climax.'

Once, when interviewed, Ian commented:

'We don't want to get diluted, really, and by staying at Factory at the moment we're free to do what we want. There's no one restricting us or the music – or even the artwork and promotion. You get bands that are given advances – loans, really – but what do they spent it on? What is all that money going to get? Is it going to make the music any better?'

If Ian hadn't argued with his manager he would have been very unusual. Musicians often behave like children and any manager will find himself acting as a father figure, solving problems and generally smoothing things out. Ian wasn't the only person to fall out with Rob Gretton, but sometimes he did react rather badly. One argument culminated in Ian stalking up and down the rehearsal room with a drum case on his head. The more he stalked the more mad Rob became and the more the rest of the band laughed. Ian's impractical approach to money always caused him difficulties. It was a concept he never understood. Once, he rang me from a hotel in the south of England. He was presented with a bill for £5 – the exact sum he had in his pocket. Furious with Rob Gretton, he blamed him for not warning him about the cost of hotel telephone bills.

'He had a lot of responsibilities, didn't he? I wouldn't count myself as any different now, because I've got responsibilities, but youth is blind. We thought, "Why doesn't he just shut up and get on with it?" That's what you do when you're young. You don't think about the ramifications.'

Peter Hook

Ian's quest for extra pocket money for himself was never ending. He even stooped to cleaning the rehearsal rooms as the rest of the band could afford to pay him. When Factory pressed the first Durutti Column album, *Return of the Durutti Column*, Tony Wilson needed someone to glue the sheets of sandpaper to the sleeves and Joy Division were drafted in. Ian did most of the job himself because the others became engrossed in the porn movie hired to alleviate the boredom and Ian needed the money for his cigarettes.

When the time came for Joy Division to start their own publishing company, it was decided to credit all the songs to Joy Division rather than any individual. The song-writing royalties were split four ways, with each person then paying Rob Gretton 20 per cent as his manager's commission. At the time I was stunned. Initially, I helped Ian financially, emotionally and practically to follow his chosen career, but when Rob started managing the band I became very much an outsider. I assumed epilepsy to be the main cause of Ian's silence, but, unknown to me, he had painted Rob a grim picture of his home life.

Yet Ian still thought enough of me to come back for consolation when he realized that the other members were not going to give him the credit he was expecting. I was out of touch with their song-writing methods and, as far as I could see at the time, Ian was a substantial contributor. As I understood it, he wrote the melodies and the lyrics – I thought he deserved at least half the credit. He was sad when he told me what had happened and although he accepted the situation, I think he must have felt he had sold out for the sake of friendship, otherwise he would not have even mentioned it. Yet, he never expressed any dissatisfaction to the band. Perhaps I was guilty of idolizing him in the same way as the press. Despite the fact that he had ceased to help in the home, to me he was still perched up there on his pedestal. When the press tried to present the band as 'Ian Curtis and Joy Division', Ian fought against it. Press interviews had always been traumatic and serious. As Ian was more approachable than the others, journalists began to ask for personal interviews.

Unknown Pleasures was released in June 1979. Packaged in a black linen-look sleeve with a white Fourier analysis in the centre, the sides were called 'Inside' and 'Outside'. 'Inside' contained 'Shadowplay', 'Wilderness', 'Interzone' and 'I Remember Nothing'. 'Outside' contained 'Disorder', 'Day of the Lords', 'Candidate', 'Insight' and 'New Dawn Fades'. The tracks 'Auto-suggestion' and 'From Safety to Where … ?' were recorded initially as part of the album, but were rejected and appeared later on Fast's *Earcom 2* with other contributions from Basczax and Thursdays.

Nearer to the truth than most people imagined, *Unknown Pleasures* was reviewed in *Sounds* under the headline 'Death Disco'. The reviewer wrote a short story around the album; his opinion was that if one was contemplating suicide, Joy Division was guaranteed to push you over the edge. Initially, I disliked *Unknown Pleasures*. This may have been owing to my jealousy at being gradually ousted from the 'tightening circle', or a genuine apprehension about the morbid dirges. As I became familiar with the lyrics, I worried that Ian was retreating to the depression of his teenage years. He had been inordinately kind to me during my pregnancy and yet these lyrics had been written at the same time.

'But I remember when we were young' – Ian sounded old, as if he had lived a lifetime in his youth. After pondering over the words to 'New Dawn Fades', I broached the subject with Ian, trying to make him confirm that they were only lyrics and bore no resemblance to his true feelings. It was a one-sided conversation. He refused to confirm or deny any of the points raised and he walked out of the house. I was left questioning myself instead, but did not feel close enough to anyone else to voice my fears. Would he really have married me knowing that he still intended to kill himself in his early twenties? Why father a child when you have no intention of being there to see her grow up? Had I been so oblivious to his unhappiness that he had been forced to write about it?

Perhaps I wasn't giving Ian the attention he required at home. Who knows? But adoration from the press doesn't seem to have been enough for him. The reviews increasingly began to dwell on Ian's distinctive dance. To me it was just part of the act and I saw my role as looking after the actor at home. I tried to provide a steady background life for him to depend on – a shelter. I was hardly likely to be impressed by his manic jerking on stage when I spent my life concentrating on eradicating the possibility of any seizures at home. Had the act become reality, or reality become the act? I endeavoured to treat him as a 'normal' person, as one should an epileptic, but he had difficulty in switching from his stage life to his home life. I could have looked after him for all time. I had been there when he was a schoolboy and yet he treated me as he might one of the sycophants who infiltrated the cushion of his friendships within the band.

Ian all but stopped talking to me and in desperation I turned to my health visitor. She was very sympathetic and arranged an appointment for me to see Ian's specialist at the hospital. Ian made it obvious he didn't want me to go and it might have been a more fruitful meeting had I gone in secret. As it was, Ian came with me. We sat in the surgery – me with Natalie asleep on my knee and Ian pouting, with his arms folded like a difficult teenager. The doctor was no help at all. I explained Ian's change in personality and all he could do was assure me that it was perfectly normal under the circumstances. I was left without a hint about how to cope with the situation and a feeling that there was something I wasn't being told. Whether the meeting would have been different without Ian's stolid presence, I do not know.

Bernard Sumner had also noticed that Ian's moods had become even more erratic: 'He had a manic personality … in his performance. If he didn't get what he wanted he could raise hell, but in a funny way sometimes.' My parents were dismayed at the opposition I was facing in trying to find out more about Ian's problems. My father was determined to get some answers for me and made an appointment with a doctor at our local practice. We felt that although medical matters are supposed to be confidential between patient and doctor, we were at least entitled to an explanation of Ian's prognosis. My father found the GP to be evasive, rude and unhelpful. He came away from the surgery insisting that the doctor himself was mad. This was not too far from the truth – within weeks the uncooperative man shot

himself. Ian reacted very squeamishly to the news, despite the fact
that he barely knew him.

For one evening at the end of July, Manchester's Mayflower Club
was renamed the Funhouse to present the 'Stuff the Superstars
Special'. The morning before this gig, Dave McCullough made the
journey to Strawberry Studios in Stockport to interview Joy Division
for *Sounds*. One pompous band member was quoted as saying: 'We
don't want to give people straight answers. We'd rather they question things for themselves.' The interview had started off well, with
Dave McCullough gleaning information about *Unknown Pleasures*
from Ian, but he was unable even to find out the names of the other
band members, let alone delve deeper into Joy Division's music.
Despite the fact that he walked away with the impression that Joy
Division were devoid of intellect, he still awarded them two pages of
undeserved publicity.

In August 1979 they played the Prince of Wales Conference Centre
at the YMCA, Tottenham Court Road. That Thursday night, Joy
Division played alongside Echo and the Bunnymen, the Teardrop
Explodes and Essential Logic. Essential Logic missed out rather as
apart from having to take the stage after Joy Division, they went on
so late that many fans were already on their way home. Adrian
Thrills in the *NME* enthused about each individual Joy Division
member in turn and finished saying: 'They have the spirit and the
feeling.' There was no doubt about it – Ian was famous. He had
achieved what he always wanted; already he was public property. I
was sick of other people making observations about Ian's personality. There was nothing left of him for me, the husband and father
ceased to exist, and any plans he made were made with Rob.

In August Ian made another appearance on the front cover of
NME, this time with Bernard Sumner. Ian was minus the raincoat
and cigarette, looking surprisingly relaxed, but Bernard's face was
turned from the camera, his tight clothing and undersized tie making
him look more schoolboyish than ever.

That same week Joy Division were booked to play at Eric's in
Liverpool. As Liverpool is my birthplace, I was looking forward to

going back immensely. I took great pleasure in driving there myself, found my own way to the club and Ian had remembered to put me on the guest list. He didn't often forget, but I was always shy about asking to get into a venue for nothing. When I went into the dressing room to look for Ian, two of the lads were in there talking to a couple of young female fans. I thought nothing of it at the time, but the day after the gig Ian asked me not to go any more unless I had the other girls with me, as it wasn't fair if I went without them. It was gradually made plain to us that wives and girlfriends were no longer welcome. It had been OK for us to boost the numbers in the audience in the early days and we had become used to sitting on the amplifiers to stop them being stolen. It was taken for granted that we would wash and iron clothes, pack cases and make excuses to employers, but now it seemed we were bad for the image. Rob Gretton shouldered the blame, but to be fair all the boys had tongues in their heads. If they had disagreed with the 'no women' policy, they could have spoken up. I was very disappointed – the whole scenario was reminiscent of when I was pregnant. Too big for my jeans, I had been panicked into borrowing a dress from my mother. That evening as Tony gave me the once over and then looked away without greeting or comment, I felt for the first time that my presence might be unwelcome or even unsuitable.

Only Steve Morris continued to take his girlfriend wherever he went. He didn't voice any objections, but just ignored what the others said. In some ways, from the point of view of managing a band, it made sense to keep their respective women away. It strengthened the relationship between the band members and allowed them to concentrate on the task in hand. If Ian was going to play the tortured soul on stage, it would be easier without the watchful eye of the woman who washed his underpants.

However, this policy helped create a rift between us. We never spoke about the easier access to drugs once the band got off the ground, but Ian knew how I felt about them. I had seen his depressive moods, knew about his earlier overdose and was aware of his apparent schoolboy death-wish. On top of all this was the questionable wisdom of mixing other substances with his prescribed drugs. When I did go to gigs, there was often a sudden silence when I walked into the dressing room. Joints were hurriedly handed back to Tony in the pretence of Ian never having touched them, and the rest of the entourage didn't comprehend my dislike of them. It never occurred to me to tell them about Ian's past – with hindsight I realize that I cherished the fact that I had known him longer too much to share it.

The Leigh Festival at the end of August 1979 was a collaboration between Zoo and Factory. It should have been a festival to remember and at the very least the first of many. I was wary of what I had been told about turning up at gigs without the other girls, so I made sure I collected Sue Sumner from her flat before driving on to the festival. It was a bright, warm day and I was disappointed because it hadn't occurred to me to take Natalie along. I mentioned this to Ian, but he was so busy discussing the size of a particularly large turd in one of the toilet tents that he didn't seem to hear me.

Thanks to James Anderton and a profound lack of publicity, the town of Leigh was closed for the day and the police presence almost outnumbered the festival-goers. After a fruitless journey into Leigh for a bite to eat, we were confronted by a road block. A short, fat thug in jeans motioned to me to stop the car and after showing me what could have been a bus pass (I wasn't allowed to read what it said), we were made to get out. While two policemen and one policewoman searched us and the Morris Traveller, the fat stupid one made jibes about the car, perhaps trying to provoke some reaction. Ian told me that someone else from Factory was in fact carrying the dope, but of course his car was not stopped. Ian and Bernard took it all in their stride.

The name Joy Division always provided a talking point for the press. Rather than make up an obscure reason for the choice, the lads remained silent. I was surprised that none of them, especially Ian, had some clever answer up his sleeve, but the lads were tired of explaining themselves. As Dave McCullough found out when he interviewed them for *Sounds* just before the 'Stuff the Superstars' gig, their attitude was one of players beginning a game in which the rules had been set out, but only the band were privy to them. Eventually they stopped giving interviews because the press tended to focus mainly on Ian and he felt he should resist that. Joy Division were in danger of being seen as a backing band when in fact the four of them made a cohesive and dynamic force.

By now, Ian was putting more of an emotional distance between us. He did bring a couple of books home about Nazi Germany, but in the main he was reading Dostoyevsky, Nietzsche, Jean Paul Sartre, Hermann Hesse and J. G. Ballard. *Photomontages of the Nazi Period* was a book of anti-Nazi posters by John Heartfield, which graphically documented the spread of Hitler's ideals. *Crash* by J. G. Ballard combined sex with the suffering of car accident victims. It struck me that all Ian's spare time was spent reading and thinking about human suffering. I knew he was looking for inspiration for his songs, yet the whole thing was culminating in an unhealthy obsession with mental and physical pain. When I tried to talk to him, I was given the same treatment as the press – a stony face and no words. The one person he did talk to about it was Bernard.

> 'Where I lived there were shelters; there was a bomb shelter in our back yard. There were underground shelters at the end of our street where we used to play. All the films on TV when we were kids were about the war. So when you grew up and understood what had gone on, you were naturally pretty interested in it … It was unfashionable to talk about it … you had to drop the subject … but I didn't think it should have been dropped and I think that was where our interest came from … It had been a decade before we were born – not that long ago.'
>
> Bernard Sumner

Bernard also remembers that Ian liked to consider Nietzsche's theory that there exists a race which is reincarnated periodically and they were the Egyptians, the Greeks, the Romans and the Nazis. However, I think Ian's obsession with the Nazi uniform had more to do with his interest in style and history. Since his infant-school days he had loved to draw soldiers from different periods – up until this point, the appeal always lay in the uniform, never warfare itself.

I also had a childhood full of wartime reminiscences. The air-raid shelters, the prefabricated houses, the holes where the iron railings used to be at the front of my grandmother's house, were there for everyone to see. I was accustomed to talking about the Second World War with my family. There was never any need for sensationalism; there was sensation enough in the facts. For me the past was a little a too close. My great grandfather was Jewish and I preferred to look at the newspaper cutting of my six great uncles who served during the war, buy my poppy and watch the Remembrance Day service every year. In the past, the only war Ian and I had discussed had been the one in Northern Ireland. He did not speak of politics, but of the romance of his ancestors being bayoneted by Black and Tans. I had no wish to reincarnate the horrors in my own mind. Ian had moved on to a higher plane by this time. If I didn't understand this sudden interest in Nazism, then he wasn't going to explain it. Band policy seemed to be interfering with our relationship. Ian regarded me with disdain, perhaps trying to ignore the fact that I had seen both sides of his personality. Much worse than his previous ambivalence towards me, I began to see in his attitude the same disdain he had shown for other members of his family.

As the pressure of playing and travelling built up through July and August, Ian's fits became more frequent and I found it increasingly difficult to communicate with him beyond finding out what kind of sandwiches he wanted. Although his doctor at the hospital changed Ian's tablets when it seemed necessary, and was apparently constantly expressing his concern about Ian's lifestyle, I found myself shut out of Ian's problems. His resentment towards me seemed to be building. Perhaps it was my imagination, but I thought he held me responsible for his condition. I knew nothing of the mental side effects of his therapy and even if I did, I would not have expected such an adverse effect on Ian's personality. As far as I was aware, his medication was being monitored and any imperfections would eventually be ironed out.

91

Ian's Aunty Nell and Uncle Ray came over from Tenerife for a month's holiday. Knowing how close Ian had been to Nell in his childhood, I decided that if anyone would be able to help me it was her. Ian's family still seemed unaware that anything was wrong and, frustratingly for me, he behaved perfectly normally at his parents' house. I took deep breaths and braced myself to bring the subject up, but was so afraid of their disbelief that I kept silent. There was never an opportunity to speak to Nell alone. On the day she left I cried. I had seen her as my last hope and was angry with my own lack of resolve.

CHAPTER NINE

THESE DAYS

The end of August 1979 was make or break time for Joy Division. They were lucky enough to be offered the chance to be support band on the Buzzcocks tour, so it was 'give up the day job' time. Ian had no qualms about this as it was what he had been waiting for. His relative contentment is borne out by the fact that he had only one *grand mal* attack during September, compared with the great number in August, when he was effectively going without sleep. I sighed with relief as this change in lifestyle should have helped Ian's affliction. The other members of the band took good care of him. Their time was spent surreptitiously watching him for signs of an impending fit and they were always there to help him recover or take him to hospital if he was particularly poorly.

To some extent Joy Division's future seemed almost rushing to greet them and in the excitement it wasn't long before Ian began to take advantage. Much to the annoyance of the rest of the band, just as they were hurtling towards fame and fortune, Ian contracted what was known as LSS (Lead Singer Syndrome). This involved disappearing into the distance while the van was being unloaded and, although he was not yet lead singer, Bernard Sumner joined in the fun. Their heads would cautiously peep around the corner to make sure the van was empty before reappearing on the scene. Anton Corbijn's photograph of the two of them carrying a flight case is indeed unique! Ian's reluctance to do any donkey work seldom caused problems as Peter Hook and Steve Morris were quite tolerant. Peter took the view that Ian was a lazy bastard and that Bernard just brought out the worst in him.

'Barney and him used to disappear and swan about like two fucking fairies. I remember going up to Barney one night, getting hold of him (the next band were on stage; he'd fucked off with Sue for a drink somewhere) and saying, "You better go and get your amp off stage." And he said, "Where is it?" The next fucking band were on and I'd left his amp on stage. I said, "I'm not fucking lifting your amp, you cunt, you can do it your fucking self." To their credit, it doesn't really matter, neither of them had much realism. I mean, Barney's really creative in the way that Ian was and maybe that's the effect it has on you. I used to be a bit different, a bit more realistic. There's a very fine line between being artistic and being a dickhead – it's like love and hate.'

Peter Hook

Futurama '79 at the Queen's Hall, Leeds, was supposed to be a sci-fi music festival, but no one seems to be able to say what made it sci-fi. Joy Division played on the Saturday (the first of the two dates) and were said by Ian Penman to be the real stars of the night. This was no mean feat, considering that seventeen bands played, including the tough competition of Orchestral Manoeuvres in the Dark and Cabaret Voltaire. Mark Johnson wrote in his book about Joy Division: 'It was one of the rare occasions that the band's wives and girlfriends were seen at a Joy Division concert.' Neither myself, Sue, nor Iris were there, so I'm not quite sure to whom he was referring.

As autumn approached they played the Factory for the last time before it closed down for an indefinite period, as the Russell Club's licence had expired. It had been 'our place' for sixteen months and there was a feeling that we were about to begin the next chapter.

When Ian felt the beginnings of an epileptic fit, he lay down on the office floor and someone was dispatched to fetch me. It was unusual for Ian to have a fit before going on stage. There were too many people buzzing around when he should have been left in peace, but Ian did manage to recover in time for Joy Division's performance. As if the evening wasn't memorable enough, there was a fracas between

94

Peter Hook and a member of the audience. Jumping down from the stage, he chased through the crowd and didn't return to play.

Mountford Hall in Liverpool was the first of the twenty-four dates that Joy Division played supporting the Buzzcocks on their autumn tour. The season began extremely well for Joy Division, who effectively blew the Buzzcocks off the stage on this first night. They earned a rave review from Penny Riley who wrote: 'It's music that washes over you, music to surrender to. Only then do you receive the maximum excitement – personal response is vital.' The Buzzcocks, meanwhile, had to make do with: 'There shouldn't have been an encore, but they did one anyway.' If further reviews are anything to go by, then by the close of the curtain on this gig, the shape that the tour was going to take had already been set.

The theme continued at Leeds University. Des Moines commented that Ian 'symbolizes Joy Division', putting the lid on the fact that whether the band as a whole liked it or not, Ian Curtis was the star of the Joy Division show. Idolaters may have loved the music, but Ian's on-stage orchestration of his own body ensured which direction they were looking towards.

Ever since I had known him, Ian had always had little catch-phrases which he insisted we both use. These seemed to me to be a kind of obsessive insurance against anything going wrong between us. For instance, 'good-bye' on the telephone could never be just 'good-bye'; it always had to be followed by both of us saying 'I love you' in exactly the same sequence. Any deviation and Ian would begin the whole process again. If I ever went anywhere on my own, the last thing Ian would say to me was, 'Watch yourself.' This wasn't to signify that I must look out for my safety, but rather that I must not speak to any other men. As the band began to be away from home, these little overprotective touches disappeared. When I asked Ian about groupies he said, 'As if I could. I'd probably have a fit.' There was no reassurance there. In fact, he turned the situation around and told me that Bernard was in the habit of bringing girls to the room for them both and pushing Ian into sleeping with them. I wasn't impressed with him trying to blame Bernard for any extra-marital sex, so typically I pressed no further. I preferred my state of ignorance.

On 16 October 1979, during a break in the Buzzcocks tour, Joy Division played Plan K in Brussels. They had understood the venue to be an oil refinery with an arts centre, but it turned out to be a sugar refinery which had been magically transformed into an arts centre by the addition of two or three bars. A hotel was not forthcoming and instead they were given cramped rooms in a hostel, where the only windows looked out on to a corridor. Yet this didn't excuse Ian's behaviour when he was unable to find the toilet. Having been caught urinating in a huge floor-standing ashtray, he proceeded to try to placate the member of staff in slow, loud English.

It is purported to have been at this gig that Ian first met Annik Honoré, though some say it was at one of the London gigs. Either way, having an attractive girl around must have provided some much-needed excitement during an arduous two months. Rather than not mention her at all, he told me about a chubby Belgian girl who was a 'tour arranger', although Steve Morris says she was posing as a journalist and she was certainly not chubby! Ian said he felt sorry for her and had taken it upon himself to act as her protector against Rob Gretton's cruel wit. Knowing Ian's caring nature, I thought nothing more about it.

During the time he spent with Annik, Ian's personality became more serious. She seemed to have quite an influence on him and almost managed to talk him into becoming a vegetarian. At home, Ian stopped sharing his life with me. Rather than tell me amusing stories and gossip, he began to name drop and use catch-phrases which meant nothing to me.

The day before the first Apollo gig, I fell down the stairs at home while carrying a kettle of boiling water up to the baby bath. I sat in the Apollo dressing room with my bandaged, scalded foot and wearing the clothes my mother had bought for me. I was totally unaware of my husband's mistress looking me up and down from across the small room. Naturally, Ian removed me from the dressing room as quickly as possible. After introducing me to a few people who seemed embarrassed and befuddled, he announced that he was going to buy a portion of chips and left me in the crowd. After the gig, I found my way backstage with the other girls.

Presumably to celebrate playing their home town, there was a party being held in one of the upstairs dressing rooms and Ian was reluctant to go. Not realizing why he had been so difficult on the first night, I decided not to go to the second gig, and Lesley Gilbert and I spent the evening at the flat she shared with Rob Gretton. I consumed a more than sufficient amount of wine, and when we telephoned the Apollo and I realized that Ian did not want to come home with me, I had even more to drink. My parents were baby-sitting and I wanted to get home at a reasonable time. Whether I was thick skinned or thick headed I'm not sure, but I couldn't believe that Ian did not want me with him. Rob Gretton managed to get Ian away from the party and Annik. He and Lesley spent the rest of the evening arbitrating between the two of us and Rob eventually persuaded Ian to go home with me. By then I was in no fit state to drive and Rob paid for a taxi to take us all the way back to Macclesfield. Neither of us uttered a word throughout the journey and it was left to me to give an explanation to my fuming parents. This was impossible for me as I didn't understand the situation myself. I still didn't know about Ian and Annik's relationship.

The signs are so obvious now that I'm embarrassed at my stupidity. The cricket match Ian went to which no one else knew about, but everyone was supposed to have played in, should have at least pointed me in the right direction. When I found Ian pressing his own trousers I should have been suspicious. I was hurt when he said he was going to see *Eraserhead* without me, but terribly worried when he didn't come home. One of his greatest fears was to be arrested for drunkenness if no one realized that he'd had a fit. I rang his parents and everyone in the band, but he was nowhere to be found. Peter Hook gave me Terry Mason's number, but by the time I dialled the digits, the line was already engaged. His father and I rang local hospitals and police stations to see if he had been taken in. When he strolled in later the next day, he was very angry that I had told any-one about his disappearance. I never found out where he'd been.

November should have been a particularly happy time for us. Ian had had only two attacks in two months and these were probably owing to the fact that he had been unable to take his tablets for a couple of days. We were relying heavily on my parents to do more than their fair share of baby-sitting and so journeys between our house and theirs became frequent. One sleeting afternoon while taking Ian on a rare visit to see my parents, I skidded on Catherine Street, right into the back of another car. We weren't going at any great speed, but it frightened Ian enough to make him curl up in a ball and hide in the foot well under the dashboard – not easy for someone who was over six feet tall.

By the end of 1979 the downward spiral of our financial situation had almost reached the bottom. Each member of the band was on a weekly wage, Ian having negotiated £15 per week. This was slightly more than the others and was given on the understanding that when the real money began to come in, Ian would pay them back. I was grateful for that concession, but it still didn't compensate for the loss of both our wages. I gather from the rest of the band that he argued frequently with Rob over this payment. From what Ian told me it wasn't the fact that Rob didn't want to part with the money, but rather that he couldn't comprehend the need for regularity. I asked around and heard that they were looking for bar staff at Silklands, a local disco. My mother offered to baby-sit while I earned some mon-ey in the evenings. As Ian had been so overly protective in the past, I thought he would try to dissuade me, but he didn't seem remotely concerned. It was just as well, as we were desperate for the money. It was a very tiring time. I looked after the baby from early in the morn-ing, worked evenings, returned home late and then waited for Ian to arrive so that I could make sure he was safe in bed. Ian was either asleep or out. It didn't matter how little money was in my purse for food, he still took it for cigarettes. My parents fed me and Natalie on Sundays when Ian was rehearsing, and took over the bills for the car, letting me use it when I needed.

Meanwhile, Joy Division continued with their support spot on the

Buzzcocks tour. Joy Division were fairly new to the type of stunts touring bands pull, so when Buzzcocks warned about tricks on the last night at the Rainbow Theatre, they took their task seriously. The Buzzcocks were tame enough to remove the battery from Steve Morris's syndrum, but Joy Division had more radical things in mind. Piles of maggots were placed on the lighting and mixing desks, every window of the crew bus was covered with shaving foam and six mice were released inside the bus for good measure. Trying to leave the theatre was also hazardous, as Joy Division circled around in Steve Morris's car throwing eggs at whoever was there. The most disgusting trick of all happened in Guildford. After removal of the fluorescent light tubes in the gents toilets excrement was smeared over the light switch and the taps.

Chris Bohn's review of the Rainbow Theatre gig accused the Buzzcocks of scuppering Joy Division's sound because they were more competition than the Buzzcocks had bargained for. Despite the vast improvement in actual sound quality when the Buzzcocks came on, it was to no avail. Joy Division had already won their audience against the odds: 'they treated their guests to a lousy sound, which dampened Ian Curtis's passionate vocals, throwing him into an uneven struggle with superior forces of technology. Inevitably, he lost, but the spirit of resistance was there.'

On 13 December 1979 my parents gave us the money to dine out. We celebrated my birthday at a small, cold Chinese restaurant in Wilmslow. Ian was miserably silent and merely ate his food in slow motion. I hadn't ordered a first course, so I sat looking at him and thinking. As a couple we had long since ceased to socialize with other members of the band and I still hadn't figured out why. Any suggestion of a night out with them was shot down, often with the excuse that Ian disliked one of the girls in particular. In fact he ridiculed her so viciously that I guessed she would be next to follow Stephanie into the cold.

Ian seemed to regard the meal as a duty, part of his function in life. I observed what a lonely couple we were and felt he must be very ashamed of me to want to keep me away from his friends. I rubbed the goose-pimples on my arms and looked back at him. His own body appeared to be unaffected by the temperature of the room. He was miles away and I wished I was too. 'Why don't you hurry? Why don't you speak?' I snapped at him. He recoiled with a startled expression as if I had struck him, then carried on eating.

The Paris gig later in December was attended by a young Frenchman called Franck Essner. After hearing 'Transmission' on the radio, he and his friends had tried to set up publication of a fanzine and intended to use this as a means of acquainting themselves with the band that wrote the song they loved so much. Towards the end of the afternoon, Franck managed to talk Rob into the idea of an interview and they exchanged addresses. Later, he sat next to Ian for dinner and they became friends.

We had Christmas dinner at my parents' house. Our late arrival and the uncomfortable atmosphere caused my family to think we had fallen out, but now I think that Ian was probably missing Annik.

The 1979 Factory New Year's Eve party took place in Oldham Street, Manchester, above a shop which was near what used to be Woolworth's until it burned down. Certain Factory bands, including Section 25, played that night to the small private audience. Ian had a particular interest in Section 25 and wanted very much to be their producer. When someone began to make a racket during their set, Ian decided to do something about it. For some reason he glanced at me before he went in punching, as if to make sure I was looking. I'd never seen him fight before and had just waded in to try to rescue him when he was knocked to the floor and kicked. The next morning, Ian's eye resembled a large blue egg. In contrast to midnight two years earlier, the New Year was not so much welcomed in as acknowledged. Most people were too busy jealously guarding their image to make any show of affection. The proceedings were dampened even further when a girl was rumoured to have had a cigarette stubbed out on her face after foolishly kissing a Certain Ration who didn't belong to her! Used to being more flamboyant on New Year's Eve, I asked Peter Hook for a kiss but he refused. In the event, the

1 Ian aged five at a railway exhibition.

2 Ian with his friend Tony Nuttall in the garden at Hurdsfield,
August 1966.

3 Ian aged eighteen.

4 & 5 Just after becoming engaged.

6 Our wedding, 23 August 1975.

7 On honeymoon, August 1975.

8 At the punk rock festival,
Mont de Marsan, August 1976.

9 Strawberry Recording Studios.

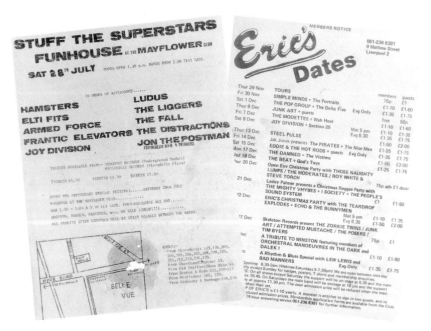

10 & 11 Liverpool and Manchester gig lists, 1979.

12 Ian photographed by Kevin Cummins.

13 Ian in concert, The Rainbow Theatre, Finsbury Park,
London, 4 April 1980.

14 77 Barton Street. 15 Ian and Natalie in South Park,
Macclesfield, March 1980.

16 In the living-room at Barton Street with Natalie. The last
picture I took of Ian, 13 May 1980.

17 Still from Anton Corbijn's 'Atmosphere' video.

closest I got to anyone at that party was when I pinched Richard Boon's bottom!

After stopping off to visit some relatives of Donald Johnson (A Certain Ratio's drummer), Donald and Tony Wilson drove Ian and me back to Macclesfield. As we passed through Prestbury – the millionaire village of Cheshire – Tony waved his arm, gesturing towards the large, salubrious houses and remarked to Ian that next year he could be living in one of them.

Realizing that something was wrong between us was the easy part. None of the literature sent to me by the British Epilepsy Association had prepared me for Ian's behaviour. I didn't know where to turn to for help or even if the epilepsy was indeed the culprit. Ian had always had an eccentric, schizophrenic personality and it was this difference which I had found so attractive in my teenage years. Now the nasty and deceitful side of him appeared to be winning. My only communication with the rest of the band was through Ian and, although he was causing them some concern too, I felt they blamed me for many of Ian's problems. People weren't as friendly as they used to be and it was understandable. Ian had fallen into a routine of telling his comrades how unhappy I was making his life and, as Peter Hook told me, putting over an uncomplimentary image. Our marriage was over and he hadn't told me.

CHAPTER TEN

I KNOW MY LIFE IS GETTING HARDER

It was January 1980 and Joy Division were about to start their European tour. Ian's case was packed and we were standing in the living room at Barton Street waiting for the rest of the lads to turn up. In Park Lane, which ran parallel to Barton Street, there was a very large house which had been converted into flats (now a hotel). As we stood there together looking out of the window, Ian suddenly suggested that we sell the house and move into one of the flats. The reason he gave was that a flat would be cheaper to maintain. I pointed out that it wouldn't be as pleasant living in a flat and that Natalie and I would be stuck there alone as he was away so much. I was a little puzzled, but it didn't occur to me that maybe he was looking forward to his share of the equity on the sale of the house. I didn't realize that he wasn't intending to move into the flat with me. He then said that Hooky had told him that he should get Natalie and I out of the house as we had no right to be there. This puzzled me as I still wasn't as conversant with my marital problems as the band were. Ignoring what was staring me in the face, I promptly forgot about his silly suggestion and asked him if I had time to nip to the corner shop for something before he left. He promised to wait until I returned, but insisted I take Natalie with me.

As I came out of the shop I saw the car coming down the road towards me. The driver slowed down as if he was going to stop to allow Ian to say good-bye (as they were going to the Continent for about ten days), but Ian's stony face turned the other way and the car carried on, just as though we had fallen out and weren't speaking. Unknown to me he was setting the scene for taking Annik on tour with him. I was genuinely surprised that he never telephoned me or even sent a postcard during the entire trip.

Ian hated travelling, but he hardly complained. He disliked his movements being restricted and his long legs would ache if he was unable to stretch them out. Rob Gretton hired a twelve-seater minibus for the band and crew, and a three-ton truck for the equipment. Luckily they crossed the Channel by hovercraft, so Ian had no need to tell anyone about his fear of flying.

The tour was particularly arduous, with a performance every night and little time to sleep, never mind recuperate. Coupled with this was the fact that Ian had brought Annik with him. Rob Gretton's reason for banning wives and girlfriends (for some reason she wasn't counted as either) dissipated rapidly, as her presence meant that Ian had less opportunity to relax with the boys. Tony Wilson remembers: 'It's always a problem in this industry – having a home life as well. What happens is that when they get a mistress or go for somebody else, far from finding somebody easier, they usually find someone harder. That was the feeling with members of Joy Division. They used to go out of the frying pan into the fire.'

When Ian came home we practically passed on the doorstep, as I was on my way to work. I had already dropped Natalie off at my parents' and whenever she was there Ian never made the effort to go and see her, even if he had been away on tour. I returned after midnight and found the house strangely quiet, but eventually located Ian lying on the floor of the blue room. He had consumed most of a bottle of duty-free Pernod and so was difficult to rouse. I was annoyed to find him incoherent and when he gained consciousness he spewed all over the carpet. He didn't raise any objections when I insisted he clean it up himself, then he sloped off to bed. I noticed weals on his body, but could not be sure if they were recent or not.

After he had gone I picked up the Bible and the knife which were lying on the floor. The Bible was still open. Chapter two of The Book of Revelation of St John the Divine was gouged from top to bottom. I read the still-legible words referring to Jezebel and flattered myself into thinking he had been worried about my fidelity while he was away. Ian had not discussed suicide with the other members of the band and neither did they know of Ian's first overdose when he was fifteen. However, he did embellish this incident and relate it to the lads. Steve Morris was suitably underwhelmed and jumped to a different conclusion than I did.

'He told us about cutting into the Bible, but he talked about it as though he'd had some strange religious experience, where I'd say he'd just got blind drunk and cut himself up. The way he told it, it was just one of those stories. It was only after he took the overdose that it turned into a chain of events. We were concerned, but no one knew what to do because we thought he was sorting it out.'

Steve Morris

'He wouldn't have told me he wanted to die young because he was my investment. He wanted to be a romantic hero and he succeeded. If Ian had lived, you would have had a tough ten years. Natalie has been deprived of a father – your life would have been hell either way. Ian got what he wanted.'

Tony Wilson

By now Joy Division fans were dressing in the same austere 1940s style – the depressives dressing for the Depression. I thought it an unlikely fashion, especially as out of necessity I was dressing dowdily myself. When Ian told me that the band were going to stop gigging for twelve months, I wasn't pleased. It was a sensible enough decision, but I knew that it would not be carried through and believed it to be a mere pacifier, designed to calm Ian down. Sure enough, an American tour was soon announced – not only that, but a string of British gigs were arranged in preparation.

I began to try to conjure up ways of drawing Ian towards me once more. Claire worked behind the bar with me at Silklands and when she threw a flat-warming party, I persuaded Ian to come with me. I was expecting Ian either to decline at the last minute or behave badly when he got there. Because most of the other guests worked at the local hospital, I thought he would deem them too ordinary for him to bother with. However, he suppressed his superior attitude and conversed with my mortal friends quite naturally. He was very charming throughout the evening.

It was daylight by the time we walked home and just as I was beginning to congratulate myself, Ian turned to me and continued a conversation which had erupted during the party. The point he wished to get across was that he wouldn't mind if I slept with another man. I walked alongside him for a while before putting it to him that if he felt like this, perhaps he didn't love me any more.

'I don't think I do,' he replied.

I moved in front of him and we carried on along the middle of Brown Street in single file. Hardly a word was spoken for the next week. Every day I wanted Ian to come up behind me, put his arms around me and tell me he hadn't meant it. After eight years of him telling me what to wear, what make-up to use and what music to listen to, I suddenly felt lost, as if I had been given my freedom and didn't know what to do with it.

Ian announced that Franck Essner was coming to stay, so any personal problems we had were pushed aside for the time being. We carried out an elaborate charade as a poor but happy family unit. During this time, Ian's attitude towards Natalie changed. He surprised and delighted me by unstrapping her from her car seat and carrying her into the house. He even allowed Franck to photograph him holding her on a visit to Macclesfield Forest. Franck had been dumbfounded at the ease of his acceptance into Ian's family.

'I arrived at Macclesfield station late one afternoon in February – Ian and your father came with me to your place. You were waiting for us with your mother, as eager and astonished at seeing a Martian as I was myself at being carried away in an ever-increasing whirl.'

The evening before Franck left, he and Ian came to Silklands just in time to meet me after working behind the bar.

'That night I finally came to the realization that Ian was

made of a different material, was just passing among us and did not belong to us. Neither did he belong to himself.'

Franck Essner

The planning for Joy Division's American tour was well under way and Ian began to think about new clothes for the trip. He persuaded me to buy some for myself by getting a store card at Top Shop and in my gullible way I allowed him to convince me that by the time the statement arrived, I would have some money to make the instalments. The shopping trip to Manchester naturally involved me using my new credit card to buy a jacket for Ian. The assistant in Top Man asked me if I was accompanying Ian to the States. I wished I was. It seemed too big an adventure for him not to share it with me and it crossed my mind that if he had still loved me, then maybe he would have asked me to go. It still hurts to know that while I was being told the band couldn't afford to take me along, Annik's expenses on the European tour had been incorporated into Joy Division's.

Strangely, shopping with him and then driving up to New Moston to visit his parents made me feel secure again. He talked of us taking a holiday together. He lied and said that Tony Wilson had offered to pay for us to go away to Holland for a few days. I began to believe that he still loved me after all, but it was only play-acting for the sake of his parents. By the time we arrived at my mother-in-law's home, I was well and truly placated and we sat calmly watching television while his mother prepared a meal. Ian assumed the cheery persona he had reserved for them since our wedding day. It was as if nothing had ever gone wrong and the fact that we had just been on a spending spree in the city gave the overall impression of well-being.

Joy Division were supported by A Certain Ratio and Section 25 at a benefit for *City Fun* fanzine at the New Osbourne Club. This gig was memorable for a few reasons, but the band's performance wasn't one of them. As it was a local gig, Ian had no way of preventing me going. Apart from driving Ian to and from the Osbourne and his appearance on stage, I didn't see him at all that evening. As I had not yet managed to 'discover' Ian's affair with Annik, the rest of the

entourage's reluctance to tell me where the dressing room was mystified me.

Sue Sumner commented on how good I looked. In fact I had
regained my figure and bought a pair of very cute, tight black jeans.
Ian's ruse to persuade me to use my credit card had not only provided him with a new jacket, but had given me a new lease of life.
Without his critical eye to discourage me, I began to blossom. Ian,
meanwhile, had his hair cut shorter and more angular, and his eyes
were tired, giving him a distracted appearance.

Reviewing the performance in *Sounds*, Mick Middles noted: 'They
have, for the time being, lost their arrogance, their urgency, their
commitment and their essential sense of feeling.'

Who can blame the band for helping Ian to cover up? I would do
the same for a friend, but perhaps the strain was beginning to take its
toll on all of them. As we left the venue, every car but mine appeared
to have been broken into.

The University of London gig, promoted by Fresh Music, was
reviewed favourably. Paul Morley led the way with his praise: 'Joy
Division's music is physical and lucid, music about uncontrollable
emotions, impulses, prejudices, fears. The group have turned inartic-
ulateness and vagueness into concrete, disturbing impressions of the
most degenerate, deepest desires … Joy Division will tear you apart.
Still.' Yet Chris Bohn was nearer to the truth when he wrote: 'Less
colourful now, they're getting closer to the despair that's been the
core of their work thus far.' If only he knew how close to the core
they were.

In spite of all the turmoil, Ian had only two *grand mal* attacks in two
months. I knew that he was taking medication for his epilepsy and
that he was seeing his specialist regularly, so I began to suspect that
something else in his life other than his illness was causing such a
dramatic change in our lives. One Sunday, while Ian was rehearsing
in Manchester, I spent the afternoon going through every pocket and
every piece of paper I could find. In the cupboard in Natalie's bedroom I found a carrier bag full of discarded notebooks. There in the
middle of an otherwise empty page, in unfamiliar handwriting, I

found the name Annik Honoré and her address in Delvino Road, London.

I had to summon immense courage to confront Ian. His depression was acute, yet he refused to tell me what was affecting his behaviour. I begged him to explain to me, but he told me he couldn't because he was afraid of what I might do. I was eager to eliminate every possibility other than the obvious. Thinking back to the days of the gay parties and remembering a fleeting glimpse of him trying on my sandals, I took a deep breath and plunged in headfirst: 'Is it a man? Have you fallen in love with a man?' Ian slid even further down in the chair, his legs splayed across the floor. His body shook with his silent laugh and I couldn't help smiling too. For those few seconds we grinned at each other and it felt good. Our eyes met in conspiracy, mutual appreciation of a private joke, as if we were a couple again. When he regained his composure and put on his serious face, I said, 'It's Annik Honoré isn't it?' and he nodded.

Ian's relief was so intense it was tangible. My reaction was to run to the blue room, break David Bowie's *Low* into pieces and then smack Ian around the head. He made no move at all. Eventually, when I asked him what he intended to do, he asked for time to break off the relationship. I agreed. I was relieved that there were no protestations of love for her and no threats to leave. I was appeased by his promise to put things right, but still kept my distance in anticipation – I wasn't prepared to lose him. He didn't ask for my forgiveness; I just assumed he would want it.

Several weeks went by and as far as I knew Ian made no attempt to tell Annik about the situation at home. I challenged him on this twice. He merely stared out of the window and up at the trees across the road. Once a fit had been induced he fell and like a fool I tried to break his fall. Pseudo-seizures can be feigned either consciously or subconsciously and are often used as a way of manipulating people. Although members of the band insist that Ian never pulled this one with them, they can't fail to have noticed the fact that he would invariably throw a fit when he was on the losing end of a dispute.

My parents didn't mind looking after Natalie while I worked, but one evening my mother decided that Ian's parents should share some of the load for a change. We also thought it would give them a more realistic view of how Ian, Natalie and I were living. Considering I had not yet told anyone about Ian's affair, this was quite perceptive of my mother.

They arrived just in time for me to put on my coat and Doreen noticed that I had taken my wedding ring off. We looked at each other. What could I do? Should I have told her that her son was in fact in London with his favourite groupie? I decided it wasn't worth the effort or the expense of my energy had I vented my anger on her. Apart from that, I didn't want to be late for work, so I went upstairs meekly and put the ring back on.

Naturally I began to take more notice of the men who were customers at Silklands. One of them was a friend of Gillian Gilbert's sister Kim. Jeff was younger than me – still in his teens, in fact. He liked the disco scene and was generally having a good time until he met me! When word got around the small town that I had found out about Ian's girlfriend, Jeff and I began to chat. A date would have boosted my confidence, but Jeff was reluctant to do anything which would interfere with my ailing marriage. Instead he became a friendly face I could talk to across the bar.

Money was extremely tight and when the red electricity bill came there was no money to pay for it. I told Ian about it but he didn't really consider it his concern. I felt ashamed at not being able to manage the money better. Ian wanted to know what I had done with the allowance we had from the band. He would bring home new clothes that Rob Gretton had bought him to wear on stage and I felt very envious of his good fortune. It didn't seem fair that he had the opportunity to travel – I loved travelling and Ian hated it. Yet I could not sympathize with him and his affluent appearance began to irritate me as our debts began to mount. I found myself keeping pathetic lists of housekeeping bills in order to prove to Ian that I wasn't spending the money on myself.

Sadly our dog had become a costly luxury. Owing to our lack of funds, even Candy wasn't getting proper food and her fur had begun to fall out. As Ian was away so much I was faced with the dilemma of needing to walk her at night-time and not wanting to leave Natalie alone in the house while I did this. Sometimes my parents were able to help out, but eventually they offered to find somewhere else for Candy to live. Ian was very distressed at this suggestion, though it didn't persuade him to come home any more often. My discovery that he carried photographs of Candy around, rather than photographs of his wife and child, made me realize how foolish I had been to carry on running his home. I knew Ian would be upset to hear that Candy had gone, but thought it cruel to keep an animal we could no longer afford to feed. Ian had ceased to make any contribution to her care and did not want to discuss or understand the problems I was having. A place was found for her on a farm in Rochdale and my parents drove her there so that I would not have to say goodbye.

Natalie was almost a year old and she constantly wanted to be cuddled and paid attention. One night, on one of the rare occasions that Ian was there at her bedtime, she refused to allow me to put her to bed. She screamed and kicked and held on to the living-room door. Determined not to let me get to the foot of the stairs, she reached out her arms towards Ian. I asked Ian if he would take her up but he said no. The screaming and crying continued, her whole body straining towards him. Eventually, I lost my temper and insisted he take her up himself. She went upstairs peacefully and fell asleep the moment Ian tucked her into her cot. I waited at the foot of the stairs for him. He returned so quickly with such an anguished look on his face that I ran up the stairs to check that Natalie was still breathing. I thought he had suffocated her. Ian's self-imposed restrictions were beginning to affect us all.

As Ian's personal life was disintegrating, his professional life was flourishing. His voice had improved. It had a powerful, enigmatic quality which would bring a poignancy to the slower songs in particular.

Closer was recorded at Britannia Row Studios, London, in March 1980 and my prayers were answered in a roundabout way in the form of a gesture from Rob Gretton. It was the only occasion I can recall when the girls were encouraged to be present. Ian grudgingly informed me that Rob had decided to send £20 to all the wives and girlfriends so that they could use it for the train fare to London to see the band during the making of *Closer*. 'I can't afford to come, can I?' I said to Ian 'Where would I sleep? I've no money for a hotel.' Ian shrugged his shoulders, omitting to tell me that two small flats had been booked for the band's accommodation and the other girls were staying there. So I sighed with relief and used the £20 to pay the electricity bill.

Sue Sumner was also unable to go to London. She always worked hard and Ian told me that she and Bernard kept their finances separate from each other. Consequently, Sue could afford to go away on holiday and was independent enough to do just that. Iris Bates (Peter Hook's girlfriend), Gillian Gilbert and Lesley Gilbert arrived at Euston Station at 9 p.m., but it was after midnight when Joy Division remembered to dispatch Steve Morris to collect them. The girls had been given the wrong telephone numbers and the whole episode resulted in none of the couples speaking to each other. Annik managed to remain concealed for the first day as one of the two flats were reserved for her and Ian, but eventually Ian made some embarrassed introductions. The next day the lads went back into the studio and the girls went window shopping because they were skint.

The rest of the band were not unduly worried by Annik's presence as they had already endured her company for the entire European tour. When faced with the prospect of booking into a hotel which doubled as a brothel, she objected on the grounds that it was immoral. The lads pointed out that it was more immoral to be 'knocking off a married bloke'. After a venomous exchange of words, she had more than earned her nickname of the 'Belgian Boiler'.

Ian seemed to be in a trance for the whole of the time he was writing and recording the lyrics for *Closer*. Wound up and intense, he was in another world. I wonder if he needed the rivalry and passion of conflict in his life to help him write the words he did.

The others carried on in the usual manner. They were so accustomed to playing jokes on each other that every time they returned to their flat in Marylebone, each of them would check their stuff, their room, their corner of the refrigerator. When Tony Wilson prepared to drive a van back to Manchester, he was given the treatment. The door handles were covered with jam and he was pelted with flour and eggs, so he had no option but to get into the van and escape.

Back in Macclesfield, I was pacing the pavements. It was lonely without Ian again and I passed my time pushing the pram around or listening to the Durutti Column's *Return of the Durutti Column*. The music was so mournful and emotional that it seemed like the only suitable thing to play. Then one day Ian rang me and in a very hushed voice said, 'It's OK, I've told her.' I dreamed about us being reunited and the future we would have together. I played the Durutti Column's sandpaper-clad album again. The nuances in the melody took a different mood and I actually danced around the house, ecstatic, believing I had somehow magically regained my husband.

Tony Wilson accompanied Annik on a train journey, during which she appeared depressed. She told Tony that she hated *Closer* because she believed Ian actually meant the lyrical content and that he was feeling the guilt as he sang. Unlike me, she had the advantage of hearing the lyrics on *Closer* before Ian's death. Although she was sensitive enough to get a hint of what was going on in Ian's mind, her warnings were ignored.

Ian came home with a cassette recording of *Closer*. Had I listened to it, maybe I too could have gained an insight into what was happening in his mind, but we didn't have a cassette player. Despite his insistence that he had told Annik it was over, she still rang, using a male friend to make the initial call. Ian refused to speak to her. When I asked to speak to her myself, the caller rang off.

CHAPTER ELEVEN

THIS IS MY CRISIS

The gigs at the Moonlight in West Hampstead took their toll on Ian. For the evenings of the 2, 3 and 4 April 1980, fans were treated to ten different acts: Section 25, Crawling Chaos, John Dowie, A Certain Ratio, Kevin Hewick, Blurt, Durutti Column, X-O-Dus, Royal Family and Joy Division. Ian's problem was that Joy Division had been billed to play every night, but at different times. On the first evening they received a rave review in *NME*, though the other acts were given the shameful label of 'a loathsome display of self admiration'. The second gig was reviewed by a different journalist who was very impressed by A Certain Ratio, but found Joy Division dull and unchallenging.

Disaster struck on the third night when Joy Division had to play with the Stranglers at the Rainbow before dashing back across London to the Moonlight. Bernard Sumner remembers: 'When I look back now, we did some gigs that we shouldn't have fucking done. He had a fit and went on and we did the Moonlight and he was really ill and he did the gig. That was really stupid.' The routine Ian had tried so hard to adhere to was severely disrupted. Lack of sleep and unusual hours destabilized his epilepsy and the fits became almost uncontrollable again. Ian was helped off stage after the fifth number, though this did not deter Neil Norman from writing that they deserved to be framed within the same context as the Velvet Underground and the Doors.

> 'When they were playing the Rainbow with the Stranglers we all went down to the Moonlight and Ian collapsed. When you're in the middle of all that you really can feel that the myth that Wilson wanted was almost there. I just think that

113

there were only two records made and it was all very small-
time for it to be the kind of myth that Wilson wanted.'

Paul Morley

'I saw three attacks and it was always two-thirds of the way
through a set. And it came to a point where in the last year,
you'd watch the group and suddenly you'd feel Ian may be
dancing great and suddenly he's dancing really great.
Hooky and Barney would be looking nervously at the stage
and you could see what was going through their minds. So I
always presumed that it wasn't because he wasn't taking the
tablets, but that he wasn't taking enough. For something was
happening within a set, doing what he did, that actually
took him to that point, that actually overcame the drugs and
made him have the attack.'

Tony Wilson

Tony Wilson was fortunate to be able to make that kind of observa-
tion. I don't remember ever seeing Ian have a fit while on stage. It
was only after his death that I found out how frequently this happened or that it even happened at all. I still feel that it was only by
eliminating my presence that he had the freedom to work himself up
into giving such a public display of his illness. It was allowed to
become an expected part of Joy Division's act and the more sick he
became, the more the band's popularity grew.

Terry Mason saw that Ian was suffering painful embarrassment at
what was happening to him. The fit at the Moonlight was particularly violent, but even so the kids in the audience thought it was an integral part of the set. Later Ian sat slumped on the bottom of the staircase that led from the dressing room to the stage. Apparently his
embarrassment was compounded when Annik was there.

'That one at the Moonlight ... he was crushed and she didn't
want to know ... he was gutted that night.'

Terry Mason

The rest of the band came home for Easter, but Ian stayed in

London with Annik, returning on 7 April, Easter Monday. I had believed the story about staying down there to work on another project outside his Joy Division commitments and was slightly suspicious when he came home with his tail so obviously between his legs. We didn't argue – I found his helplessness infuriating. He seemed able to surrender control of his life as if it was nothing to do with him at all.

That evening he came up to bed and announced that he had taken an overdose of Phenobarbitone. I called an ambulance and he was taken to hospital to have his stomach pumped. Again, I didn't tell my family because I was afraid he would leave me for good. I decided that the best person to tell was Rob Gretton. I didn't know how ill he had been over Easter and had no idea what prompted his suicide attempt. Whether it was a threat or a cry for help, I didn't know how to help him. I thought maybe Rob could cancel some gigs and force Ian to stay at home and rest. He had left a suicide note. It said that there was 'no need to fight now' and to 'give his love to Annik'.

Tony Wilson, his then wife Lindsay Reade and Alan Erasmus came to the house the next morning. Lindsay stayed to look after Natalie. I was too ignorant of the situation to be as distraught as I should have been. Lindsay says she noticed my strength at that time. I feel my detachment and state of shock was mistaken for stoicism, giving me an air of being too practical to comprehend the kind of suffering Ian was feeling. No one realized that, being left out in the cold, I was also very much in the dark. I hadn't been allowed to gigs, so I hadn't heard any of the songs written since *Unknown Pleasures* – neither had I delved into Ian's lyric sheets nor even been able to listen to a cassette tape. They may have pitied me for what I was going through, but they had no idea how it felt to suffer something and not know what it was.

Tony asked me if there was anything to drink. I thought it a strange request, but when Lindsay poured a small whisky it was handed to me. I felt too agitated to drink it, nobody seemed to be saying anything and although Tony took command, he seemed uneasy with the role. I watched him read Ian's suicide note and put it in his pocket – perhaps for Annik, perhaps in order to remove any evidence.

Eventually Tony and Alan took me to the hospital to see Ian. I sat in the car with them while Tony explained to me that musicians were renowned for having a multitude of simultaneous relationships and it was something I would have to come to terms with. Tony even suggested that I look for someone else myself. I never understood why I was given that little lecture – it hadn't been me who had just taken an overdose and as I discovered later it was Annik who Ian had been having problems with. I suppose Tony was guessing at events and reasons and trying to equate Ian's problems with his own life. I thought that if I kept my head down and tried not to pressurize Ian he would come running back to me and our marriage. I hoped that what I thought was a deep friendship could revert to normal. Unwittingly, I was aiding the perpetuation of the myth that our marriage had been long over before the destructive policies of 'the band' began to erode and eat away into our relationship. The music business makes a jealous mistress and although Joy Division slipped easily into the role of family and friend, unfortunately for Ian none of the band could be his wife. Ian's choice of Annik as concubine was disastrous as she was unable or unwilling to give him comfort after he'd had an epileptic fit. Her embarrassed rebuffs hurt him deeply.

Ian was seen by a psychiatrist during his overnight stay and was judged not to be suicidal. Lindsay drew a picture for Ian as he sat in the visiting room. Beneath it she quoted the words of David Hare: 'There is no comfort. Our lives dismay us. We have dreams of leaving and it is the same for everyone I know.'

I'm sure we all have dreams of leaving at some time in our lives, but when we reach the bottom, most of us go running home. Where else is there when we need help? Yet Ian didn't run to his friends or his family. At this stage, even his parents had no idea of his misery. I don't possess enough fingers to count the number of hurt people who believe they could have helped if only he had approached them. He must have felt an acute sense of loneliness, a disabling inability to communicate and surrender to treatment. How unhappy does one have to be before living seems worse than dying? It might have been useful if I had known that suicide was five times more common among epilepsy sufferers.

Tony insisted on speaking to Ian alone. I don't know what was said, but Ian came home only to collect his clothes. He told me that the doctor had suggested he stay somewhere quiet, where there were no children. Although Ian's medical records show him as being discharged to go home, he was taken to Tony's cottage in Charlesworth, near Glossop. I was instructed by someone at Factory not to telephone him as he needed rest. That was easily done – I had not been given a contact number. My husband, my child's father, had effectively been removed from our lives and we had no way of getting in touch with him.

Ian told Peter Hook about the overdose: 'I was fucking pissed, just fucking around.'

> 'An uncle of Iris's is a copper and he said that they were passing round Ian's case history as a perfect example of a schizoid depressive, to teach coppers that this is how a schizophrenic ... If it was that much of a classic case, you'd think they could have sussed it out and put you right.'
>
> Peter Hook

There was no respite from touring. Ian went straight from his suicide attempt to a gig at Derby Hall, Bury, on 8 April 1980. Rob Gretton insisted that the gig went ahead even without Ian, who stood in the wings unable to sing. He told Lindsay Reade that he had a sensation of looking down on the gig and the band, and that it was all carrying on without him, which it was.

The band were torn between going on stage and calling the gig off, but a decision had to be made quickly. I doubt whether the outcome would have been any different if they had just packed up and sneaked out of the back door – although it might have alleviated the stress Ian was feeling.

'Rob said there was no point in doing the gig and we ended up with a complete riot. At the time, doing the gig probably seemed more important than it was. Ian and Rob wanted to do the gig, but I didn't. I thought that if there was something wrong, doing the gig wasn't going to sort it out. That was terrible, but I remember thinking at the time that he would probably do it again and that's why I thought we should sort it out.'

Steve Morris

The fury of the audience began to build up as Factory performed in a sort of rota, swapping around band members, and Ian sang only two numbers. Disgruntled fans began throwing things at the elaborate glass ceiling lights. The fragments rained down on the band so they went off stage, leaving the road-crew to try to protect the equipment. After two pint pots hit the stage, Rob Gretton launched himself into the crowd. Five people needed hospital treatment, including Twinny, Joy Division's roadie, who was smashed over the head with a castellated pot while attempting to rescue Rob Gretton. Ironically, Factory Records had paid Harry Demac to make a four-track recording of the whole sorry pageant. When the shouting was over, Tony Wilson found Ian sitting upstairs in the side bar, crying. Tony consoled him by reminding him of the riot at the Free Trade Hall, Manchester, when Lou Reed had refused to do an encore.

'I said, "I went to a gig where there was a riot, the best gig I've ever been to – the Lou Reed gig at the Free Trade Hall." And he looked up ... his eyes ... he says, "The fucking riot!" I said, "Exactly, man, it was wild." There it was – he was a fan of Lou Reed.'

Tony Wilson

Sadly, Tony Wilson was still oblivious to the depth and nature of Ian's depression. The only way to cheer Ian up momentarily was to equate him with one of his heroes. Ian was living in fairyland and in our own way we all helped him to stay there.

Tony didn't spend much time at home during that week, but

before he left for work he placed pieces of blue paper in a volume of W. B. Yeats, so that Ian could refer to certain poems. It was Lindsay who had the unenviable task of looking after Ian. He ate mechanically and paid little attention to anything until she began to tell him of her interest in hypnotism. He responded to this idea and wanted to try it. He went under very easily, but unfortunately Lindsay had not had any instruction as to what to do once he was in a trance. She asked him how he felt and he replied that he felt confused.

Ian had already been hypnotized a couple of times by Bernard Sumner, who also found Ian a compliant subject. Bernard had quite long conversations with Ian while he was in this hypnotic state and one of them was recorded on a cassette. Ian had brought it home for me to listen to on a borrowed cassette player. Although the words were mumbled and quiet, Ian insisted that each time he was hypnotized he had regressed to a previous life and for those few minutes, Ian believed he was an old man on his death bed.

On 11 April 1980, when Joy Division played the reopened Factory Club, it was the first time I had seen Ian since he had gone to live with Tony Wilson. The brawl in Bury had panicked Rob Gretton into arranging back-up protection for the entourage. His friends Korky and Robo, who were bouncers at Chequers Disco in Altrincham, were drafted in to help. (They eventually became the Haçienda's first bouncers.) To Terry Mason Ian appeared unruffled, if a little apologetic, as it had been Terry and Twinnie who had suffered most at the previous gig.

The atmosphere was strained, but Ian did make an effort. He sat with me and bought me a few drinks. All the same, nothing was said about what had happened or how long he intended to stay at Tony's. It was crowded in the bar and I had hoped for a more intimate meeting, but after a short while it was time for him to join the rest of the band.

When he left, I began to talk to the other girls. No one had rung me to see how I was – I suppose because they were embarrassed. Yet now they began to tell me what had happened in London while *Closer* was being recorded. It was then I found out that while Ian had allowed me to worry about money and accommodation, two flats had been booked. The majority had been squashed in one flat, while Ian and Annik enjoyed the luxury of space for themselves. I was told he behaved in an obsequious manner towards her and she in turn ordered him about like an obedient little dog. I had a few more drinks and by the end of the set I was beside myself with jealousy, humiliation and anger. To say I was miserable is to put it mildly.

Ian was already downstairs. I followed him down and tried to attract his attention. I don't know if he knew what was coming or if he had already decided to ignore me, but I played right into his hands and threw my handbag at him in temper. He blinked and carried on talking. Someone whispered to me that Ian had intended coming home with me that night, but had consequently changed his mind. The frustration was intolerable. I was desperate for any kind of communication. I was still too much in love to think about ending the marriage for myself. Tony was heard to tell Ian to 'rise above it'.

I drove away from the club alone – by coincidence, in parallel with Tony's car, now loaded up with various Certain Ratios and Ian. As we reached a roundabout the two cars parted and we were taken in different directions. Ian stayed with Tony Wilson for almost another week.

Natalie's first birthday was on 16 April 1980 and I was saddened that Ian still hadn't come home. My mum made a cake and we had a small party without him. I could hardly believe that he had forgotten his daughter's birthday, but still did not confide in my parents. As far as they were concerned, Ian was working.

Understandably, towards the end of the week Lindsay began to feel depressed herself. Ian's inanimate state was more than she could bear and she vented her feelings by screaming and shouting at Tony that Ian had not moved all week. Tony didn't appreciate that Ian needed specialist help and took the view that Ian and Lindsay were both 'nutters' who were driving each other round the bend by being together in the house all day.

When Tony and Lindsay came back from a short trip to Stratford, Ian had left. He returned briefly the following Monday to pick up some clothes that Lindsay had washed for him. She tried to impress upon him that he could stay, but he wouldn't. He seemed unaware of all the people who were trying to help him. Rather than appreciate Lindsay's attempt to provide the time and space for him to think, he came home and sulked because they had gone out for a day. He complained: 'Tony left me with a pile of Hendrix LPs and some dope.'

Grateful for his return, I was afraid to try to discuss anything and to some extent he appeared more like his old self. We were still stony-broke, but he suggested that during this 'calm' period we go for another Chinese meal in Alderley Edge. This time we were able to talk. Ian complained about hangers-on and the difficulties of being on the road. I told him not to worry about me because I had already begun making a new life for myself. I told him I had made new friends and that I would be able to cope while he was away on tour. He wasn't taken aback, but warned of the danger of letting people get too close. He said there were people who, once they had a hold of you, would not let go. I took this to mean Annik in particular, but talking to the band one gets the distinct impression that Ian was more susceptible to hangers-on than the rest of the lads.

The video for 'Love Will Tear Us Apart' was recorded on 25 April 1980. Anything to do with Ian's personal life had been put on hold, yet there was always plenty of time to arrange recordings and gigs for the band. No matter how he felt inside, to the onlooker he had become a music-business puppet.

The one good thing to come out of Ian's attempted suicide was that an appointment was made for him to see a psychiatrist at Parkside Hospital. Amazingly, when the day came for Ian's visit to the psychiatrist, we went together. On the way there he told me how unhappy he was in the music business. He said that when 'Transmission' and *Unknown Pleasures* had been released, he had achieved his ambitions. Now there was nothing else left for him to do. All he ever intended was to have one album and one single pressed. His aspirations had never extended to recording 'Love Will Tear Us Apart' or *Closer*. As I drove along, he told me how he wanted to leave Joy Division and join a circus. I comforted myself with the knowledge that we were on our way to visit the psychiatrist and shrugged off the wider implications of having a husband who wanted to act out the cliché of 'running away'. He had also told Steve Morris of his desire to leave, but Steve was under the impression that Ian wanted to live in Holland.

It felt strange going into the gates of Parkside Hospital. It seemed not to have changed in all the years since I had worked there as a schoolgirl – now here I was taking my own husband into the building. When we reached the hospital reception, Ian was embarrassed. He had misread his appointment card and turned up about two weeks early. His next visit would be very different.

CHAPTER TWELVE

DECIDE FOR ME

As I had suspected, the suggestion that Joy Division would cut down on gigging for a while didn't come to much. Throughout April and May 1980, they always seemed to be busy playing or rehearsing when I especially thought they should have been resting for the forthcoming American tour, so when Ian said he was going away for a break I wasn't surprised. He said he'd chosen to stay in a small pub in Derby and I asked him if I could go with him. He explained gently that he needed time alone and I accepted this.

He'd only been gone for two days when I began to wonder. It struck me that, yet again, I had no way whatsoever of contacting him, so I rang Rob Gretton to see if he had left a telephone number. Rob seemed annoyed with me. 'What is it with you two?' he said. 'Can't you talk to each other?' I was devastated. His exasperation had obviously got the better of him and he sounded so annoyed that I was hurt by the tone of his voice. All I really wanted was for someone to tell me what was happening. I hung up – the secret had festered long enough. Unable to stand the loneliness, I telephoned my parents. By the time Rob tried to ring me back, I had left the house.

In fact Rob was short tempered because Ian and Annik had been sitting in his and Lesley's flat when I rang. They'd run out of money and landed themselves on his doorstep, asking him to solve their financial problems. Ian had suddenly gained an insight into how it felt to have no money at all. It still irritates me intensely that this fact had eluded Ian for so long.

The next morning my father rang Ian's parents and told them what had been happening. They were astonished as they'd had no idea that we'd been having problems. Annik caught the train back to

London and the episode culminated in Ian's parents, Rob and Lesley watching Ian pace up and down our living room in Barton Street. He refused to speak to anyone. I knew he would be angry with me because I had 'told' or 'informed' on him to our parents, as we had an unspoken agreement to keep it all a secret and sort it out between ourselves, like naughty children.

I took it for granted that once the secret was out I would lose him for ever, but it was different now. It was clear I would have to lose him in order to start living again, and deep down inside he must have wanted to lose me too. I suddenly felt angry with Annik. She had a sexy accent, a job at the Belgian embassy and seemingly enough time and money to follow Joy Division around Europe. I felt that as Ian's wife and the mother of his child I deserved more status, but it hadn't worked out like that. I had been well and truly ousted. In an attempt to redress the balance I rang her at the embassy and screamed at her that I was divorcing Ian and would be naming her as co-respondent. She falteringly replied that she would do whatever I wanted. Having worked at Macclesfield county court, I regarded being named as co-respondent terribly shameful.

It was difficult initiating the divorce, but once I had made the decision it felt wonderful. It seemed as though a huge weight had been lifted off my shoulders. For that short time, I honestly believed that Ian was not my problem any more. As far as I was concerned, I could leave Rob, Tony and Annik to try to sort out Ian's life. I believed I had done him a favour by eliminating one of his biggest worries – me. If Ian didn't have the guts to concede the end of our relationship, I did. I admitted to myself that I had made a hash of my life and began to make plans to wipe the slate clean and start again. I borrowed a dress from my sister, rang Jeff, told him what had happened and arranged a date for that very evening. At the age of twenty-three, for the first time in my life, a man called for me in his car and took me out for a drink. It felt fantastic. I was young and I began to feel wanted again. He treated me as a human being, a feeling person and provided the much needed shoulder to cry on. Not that we had a wonderful or romantic time, as I needed to talk and couldn't help discussing the previous events. He was there to listen.

One of the girls tried to persuade me to drop the divorce application. She told me I should hang on for a while as Joy Division were about to make a fortune and it would be more lucrative to divorce Ian when he was rich. I decided my pride was too valuable an asset.

Ian stayed with Bernard Sumner and his wife for a short time. To Sue Sumner he appeared quiet and depressed, but he did talk to Bernard a great deal. When Bernard commented on how fortunate it was that he had not gone through with his suicide bid, Ian said, 'I didn't go through with it because I heard that if you didn't have enough tablets you get brain damage.'

Ian would stay up very late at night while he lived with Bernard and Sue, but that was something he had always liked to do. He suffered from dizzy spells and a rash, which may have been shingles. Talking was useless. He would agree with whatever anyone said and then fall into another depression.

Before Ian died, he returned to live with his parents for a while. Even before his illness, Ian had never been mentally equipped for living alone. He had lived with his parents up until our marriage and afterwards with friends. Daily, routine life never touched him. Although he seemed to enjoy solitude, it was not a state in which he could exist as he was incapable of fending for himself. It's not surprising that the restrictions of epilepsy depressed him and exaggerated his dependency on others.

Eventually it was time for Ian to attend his psychiatrist's appointment. This time Terry Mason was dispatched to drive Ian and Rob Gretton rang to tell me so that I could be there. Terry was shocked at my arrival at the hospital, but I felt I owed it to Ian to make this one final attempt to help him. I requested to see the psychiatrist alone, before Ian's appointment, as I didn't see how he could be properly assessed if no one knew the details of his behaviour. I tried to explain coherently what had been happening in our lives – the lies, the contradictions – but by now I was weeping uncontrollably. My wailing and raving made it seem as if I was the one who needed treatment.

To make matters worse, when Ian entered the room he was so cool and calm one would have thought we had never met before. When asked if he was going to return to live with me he replied: 'I might, I might not.' I left the room and sat outside with Terry. This was Ian's chance to break down and tell a professional how he really felt. This was the best opportunity he'd had to get help.

When Ian finally came out he looked down at me with all the hate in the world and said, 'I'm never coming home.' I thought he was referring to the fact that I had brought his behaviour and his illness out into the open, that he believed I had betrayed him and his staying away was my punishment. I was sorry for him and completely help-less. I couldn't understand why he wasn't taken into hospital where he could be put under the care of one professional person, rather than be pulled in different directions by a bunch of amateurs. I began to question my own sanity, to wonder if perhaps I was the one who needed help. I thought people might see me as the jealous wife, insisting that her husband was mentally ill because he had dared to find another woman. The hierarchy at Factory made me feel like some kind of obstruction to Ian's imminent fame and, more impor-tantly, fortune.

Joy Division played their final gig on 2 May 1980 at High Hall, Birmingham University. It was there that Tony Wilson had his last conversation with his protégé. They discussed what Tony considered to be Ian's tendency to use 'archaic English language and nineteenth-century grammatical constructions'. Talking like two elderly scholars was one way of avoiding the real-life issue. Perhaps this helped to take Ian's mind off his personal problems, but the climax to the sce-nario could only be postponed, not cancelled altogether.

Rob Gretton tried to forestall any difficulties that may have come up during the American tour by appointing Terry Mason as Ian's minder. It would have been Terry's job to look after Ian, making sure he took his tablets, didn't drink and got plenty of sleep. All the fun and games bands on tour have would have been out of bounds for him.

Three months in hospital would have been a better idea. When someone close to you needs that kind of help, it's very difficult to recognize and even harder to admit. Any attempts to change the direction in which Ian was going would have been thwarted by his inability to accept responsibility for his own actions. No matter whom Ian was speaking to at the time, he was always able to name a scapegoat for his problems. Unable to face making decisions himself he asked friends, notably Bernard Sumner, what he should do. Quite rightly Bernard declined to choose between Annik and myself on Ian's behalf. Bernard also walked Ian through a cemetery one day and pleaded with him to realize that this was where he would have ended up had his first suicide attempt succeeded.

Ian would have made a gifted actor. He convinced us all that the conflicts in his life were caused by outside influences and that the stress he was suffering was a direct result of the lifestyle he was leading. Truly, as his own judge and gaoler, he had engineered his own hell and planned his own downfall. The people around him were merely minor characters in his play.

Ian had his last appointment at the epilepsy clinic on 6 May 1980. As fate would have it, he saw a different doctor than usual and left an overall impression of a man who was finally getting his life together and looking forward to the future. Terry Mason and Rob Gretton accompanied Ian to Macclesfield on this occasion and he brought them to the house to collect a few things. He gave Terry Mason much the same impression that he gave his doctor that day. He told Rob and Terry that he had sorted everything out and we were going ahead with the divorce. He gave Terry a sleeve for his copy of *An Ideal for Living* as he didn't have one. Terry was also offered some of Ian's records, including his copy of the Sordide Sentimentale single 'Atmosphere'/'Dead Souls', which had the serial number 1106. Ian's sudden whim to give away his possessions might have provided a clue to his intentions, but his generosity had been legendary in the past and could sometimes be overwhelming if he was in the right mood.

Living with his parents and having little or no contact with me must have been good for him, because he had not had a fit in four

weeks. On Tuesday 13 May, Ian came to Macclesfield to see me and
Natalie. When I came home he had already let himself into the house.
He had washed up and put fresh irises and freesias in his blue room
where he used to do his writing. I was puzzled rather than pleased
and thought this would be the last time I saw him before he went to
the States. I also thought Joy Division would be hugely successful
there and that Ian would forget about his family in Macclesfield.
Before he left I insisted on taking one last photograph of Ian with
Natalie. She lay on her changing mat kicking her legs and rather than
pick her up, he leant down and put his face next to her. The picture
shows him pale and haunted. When I collected the photographs from
the developers after Ian's death, that shot was missing and I had to
ask them to reprint it.

Ian, Bernard and Paul Dawson (an old friend of Bernard's) played
pool in a pub in Manchester on the following Thursday. Paul, the
Amazing Noswad, would-be magician, was able to make Ian laugh.
It was the first time Bernard had seen him laugh in a long time, so it
was arranged that they should all meet again on the Saturday.

Peter Hook saw Ian on Friday, when he dropped him off at his parents' house. They both spoke excitedly about the American trip.

> 'He killed himself on Saturday night. I couldn't believe it. He
> must have been a pretty good actor. We didn't have a bleed-
> ing clue what was going on. You tried to help him with your
> limited experience and you did what you could, but as soon
> as you left him he went back, you know?'
>
> Peter Hook

Rather than ringing to confirm the Saturday arrangements, Ian
rang Bernard and said, 'I can't make it. I'm going to see Debbie, I
want to talk to her. I won't be able to make it. I'll see you on Monday
morning at the airport.' He sounded calm and Bernard wasn't worried about him, but that was the last time they spoke to each other. I
also heard that he told Rob Gretton he was coming to Macclesfield to
watch a film on TV which he felt would upset his father if he watched
it with him. This turned out to be *Stroszek*, a Werner Herzog film

about a European living in America who kills himself rather than choose between two women. The last line of the film talks of a dead man in the cable car and the chicken still dancing, which is why the run-offs to *Still* include 'The chicken won't stop', 'The chicken stops here' and chicken footprints walking between the grooves.

'The week before, we went and bought all these new clothes; he was really happy.'

Rob Gretton

'I don't think Ian was worried about the American tour.'

Bernard Sumner

'If he was depressed, he kept it from us.'

Steve Morris

I believe Ian chose his deadline. It was important to keep up the charade in front of the band in case they tried to dissuade him. The only reason he was no longer worried about the American trip was because he knew that he wasn't going.

CHAPTER THIRTEEN

MY TIMING

I recall the events of that final weekend and it's as if I am watching a video that someone else had produced in my absence. I have run it through so many times, looking for a point to break and insert some other sequence of events. I do know I am not the only person to feel like this, to spend time thinking 'if only', making the mistake of believing there was one single action which could have saved Ian's life. Now I am grateful he died at home and not while he was on tour in America. Tony Wilson was quoted in *Select* magazine as saying, 'Ian Curtis's death was the worst thing that ever happened to us. If only he'd survived for another thirty-six hours and got to America.' In reality, Ian looked towards that particular trip with some trepidation. He feared the American reaction to his epilepsy in certain States and he was terrified of flying. He longed to travel by ship, but mentioned it to no one but me, as he knew this was an illogical and impossible idea. I don't believe he had any intention of going to America. If he had, I doubt if 'being there' would have prevented his suicide.

That weekend was particularly busy for me. There was the usual disco on Friday night, a wedding reception on Saturday afternoon and a further disco for the wedding in the evening. I was pleased to have the opportunity to earn more money. Then Ian rang unexpectedly and announced he would be coming 'home' on Saturday before flying on Monday. Sunday was to be the only day I had free that weekend and although I was apprehensive about seeing him again, I thought perhaps his visit indicated a desire to talk. I'm not sure Ian understood why I was working as a barmaid and waitress. Rock stars jetting to the States to make a living was far removed from the existence I had led for the previous year.

I was behind the bar until after midnight on Friday 16 May and also worked the lunchtime bar on Saturday. I slept at my mother's house because Natalie was staying there. During my afternoon break I rested and then went down to see Ian before starting work again for the evening. I explained to him what my work situation was and that Natalie would be sleeping at my parents' house that night. 'Why don't you bring her here?' he said, 'She'll be OK with me.' I tried to reason with him. It seemed such a simple request, but I didn't trust him. Eventually, my mother helped me by making the decision for me and we kept Natalie away. Ian said he wanted to talk to me and I promised to go back after work.

A friend's sister was married that day, so there were people I knew at the wedding reception who asked me how Ian and I were. I nodded and smiled: everything was fine; yes, everything was just wonderful. I was eager to keep up the charade, not wanting to tell a wedding party that my own marriage had failed. I collected glasses, stepped over extended legs and dodged waving arms, with my own limbs aching and my head pounding.

In the early hours of the morning in Barton Street, Ian had been watching the Werner Herzog film. When I arrived he had almost finished a large jar of coffee and was helping himself to another mug of the thick, black mixture. He asked me to drop the divorce and I argued that he would have changed his mind by morning. There was no talk of love that night – the last time it had been mentioned was when he told me that he didn't think he loved me. He told me he had spoken to Annik earlier that evening. Their relationship was still very much alive and I began to feel extremely weary – our conversation was going around in circles.

Ian was afraid I would meet another man while he was away. As he became more unreasonable I was convinced he was going to work himself up into a fit, so I offered to spend the night with him. I drove to my parents to tell them what I was doing, but when I returned to Ian he had changed his mind again. This time he wanted me to stay away altogether. I could tell by his face that the fit wasn't going to surface. He made me promise not to return to the house before 10 a.m. as he was catching the train to Manchester then. Any other night and I might have stayed to argue with him, but I was exhausted and relieved that I was allowed to leave.

I drove the Morris Traveller along Bond Street. Ian would be OK; he always was. I had spent too many nights sitting up with him. It was time to look after Number One.

After I had gone, Ian made himself still more coffee. In the pantry was the all-but-empty whisky bottle from which he squeezed every last drop. He listened to Iggy Pop's *The Idiot*. He took Natalie's photograph down from the wall, retrieved our wedding picture from the drawer and sat down to write me a letter. It was a long, very intimate letter in the same sprawling capitals he used to write his songs. He did say he wished he was dead, but didn't actually say that it was his intention to kill himself. He talked of our life together, romance and passion; his love for me, his love for Natalie and his hate for Annik. He couldn't have hated Annik. I never heard him say he hated anyone. I think he wrote that to try to please me. He told me he couldn't bring himself to be so cruel as to tell her he didn't want to see her again, even to save his marriage. The pages were full of contradictions. He asked me not to get in touch for a while as it was hard for him to talk to me. By the time he had finished writing, he told me, it was dawn and he could hear the birds singing.

I crept into my parent's house without waking anyone and was asleep within seconds of my head touching the pillow. The next sound I heard was: 'This is the end, beautiful friend. This is the end, my only friend, the end. I'll never look into your eyes again ... ' Surprised at hearing the Doors' 'The End', I struggled to rouse myself. Even as I slept I knew that was an unlikely song for Radio One on a Sunday morning. But there was no radio – it was all a dream.

As it was well past 10 a.m., nearly midday, I dressed and prepared to take Natalie home. My mother offered to come with me, but I refused, confident that Ian would not be there. The curtains were closed. I could see the light bulb shining through the unlined fabric. Thinking Ian might still be asleep, I left Natalie in the car and waved to Pam Wood cleaning her windows. He could have overslept – a chance to talk in the daylight, when I wasn't tired, when he was calm. Yet, as I stood in the hall somehow I knew he had never gone to bed.

I didn't call his name or go upstairs. At first I thought he had left because the house smelled strangely fresh. The familiar clinging stench of tobacco wasn't there. He must have caught the train after all. There was an envelope on the living-room mantelpiece. My heart jumped when I realized that he had left a note for me. I bent forward to pick it up and out of the corner of my eye I saw him. He was kneeling in the kitchen. I was relieved – glad he was still there 'Now what are you up to?' I took a step towards him, about to speak. His head was bowed, his hands resting on the washing machine. I stared at him, he was so still. Then the rope – I hadn't notice the rope. The rope from the clothes rack was around his neck. I ran through to the sitting room and picked up the telephone. No, supposing I was wrong – another false alarm. I ran back to the kitchen and looked at his face – a long string of saliva hung from his mouth. Yes, he really had done it. What to do next? I looked around the room expecting to see Ian standing in a corner watching my reaction. My instinct that he was playing a cruel trick. I had to tell someone. I opened the front door and saw Mr Pomfret going through his back gate. My lips opened and I mouthed his name but the words wouldn't come. I turned to Pam and Kevin – they were still outside. Pam heard the urgency in my voice and ran to me, but I couldn't tell her. What if it hadn't really happened? Supposing I had imagined it? Kevin pushed past me to the kitchen and back again. In slow motion Pam lifted Natalie from the car, handed her to me and ushered us both along the road to their house.

The police asked me to formally identify the body, but eventually my father was allowed to do it instead. I regret that very much. I sat in the car and waited – still too shocked to cry, but able to notice that, yes, like the old cliché, the sun was still shining and the breeze was still blowing. It was a beautiful day. The green leaves above Barton Street buffeted against a blue, blue sky. For the last time Ian and I were driven in opposite directions. I was to hear later at the inquest that Kevin Wood and another young man from the street had tried to cut Ian down before the police arrived. This had been a harrowing experience – there wasn't a sharp knife in the house.

Pat O'Connor was by then head porter at Macclesfield District and General Hospital. When he was called in to book in the latest corpse he was shocked to see his old friend Ian Curtis. It was his job to escort Ian's body and the police down to the morgue. A few days later my parents and I returned to the house to collect a few clothes and toys. My father dismantled the clothes rack and chopped it into tiny pieces. I noticed the record player was switched on and, lifting the lid, I saw *The Idiot* still turning. While I was there, it struck me that Ian had brought none of his usual medication which had been essential to his well-being. I did find a Dictaphone which the band had given Ian to hum his melodies into. There was only the tape that was in it – it was blank.

It was some time before I was allowed to go to the police station to read the letter which Ian had left for me. I was handed the original and despite the private nature of the letter, my mother was handed a typed transcript to read. I was a little surprised at this, but didn't feel as uncomfortable as she did.

Rob Gretton rang me before the funeral to ask when he could arrange for Annik to visit the Chapel of Rest to see Ian's body. I was upset, but we did come to an arrangement and Tony Wilson took it upon himself to make sure Annik didn't appear at the funeral and cause a scene. Even after his death we were jostling for possession, importance, affection – call it what you will. Rumour has it that Annik was already wending her way back up north before she knew of Ian's death.

> 'That's what I heard, that was part of the reason why ... I gathered that that was part of the reason why he thought this was the only way out. He didn't know how to handle it.'
> Lindsay Reade

Annik stayed with Tony Wilson and Lindsay Reade for a week, sleeping in the same room where Ian had slept. She sat on their floor, crying and playing Joy Division records for twenty hours of every day she was there. Annik showed Lindsay a letter that Ian had written to her. It began 'Dear Annik, It was really painful hanging there'. Presumably he meant on the other end of the telephone.

They took Annik with their floral tributes to the Chapel of Rest before the funeral. Tony's car was a Peugeot estate and had always been known to Lindsay, ironically, as 'the hearse'. Once in the Chapel of Rest, they were able to see the marks on Ian's neck. Alan Erasmus leaned forward and moved Ian's clothing to cover the marks before his parents came to view the body. Tony's words to Ian's corpse were, 'You daft bugger!' He said to me later, 'I've always felt a friendly annoyance that he fucked off.'

Tony Wilson also took Paul Morley to the Chapel of Rest, but Paul declined to go in. He felt his relationship with Ian had not been close enough to be able to view his body. The event also must have dredged up overwhelming emotions as his own father had committed suicide. Tony Wilson's main reason for inviting Paul Morley was Tony's intention that Paul write 'the book', but he was affronted and turned down the offer.

Factory Records held their own wake for Ian and spent it smoking dope and watching the film *The Great Rock'n'Roll Swindle*.

Ian was cremated on 23 May 1980. I remember the rawness in his mother's voice and the blank, staring faces of the remaining band members. I felt the shame of failure and the bitterness of seeing them all there, sharing my grief when it was too late. Only the family and our friend Kelvin Briggs were invited back to my parents' house. Kelvin took care of me that day, just as he had taken care of Ian on our wedding day. After a couple of whiskies my nerve cracked. As I began to laugh with embarrassing hysteria, I looked up at Kelvin's face to see the tears rolling silently down his cheeks.

CHAPTER FOURTEEN

WRITTEN THERE FOR ALL

The inquest was scheduled for Friday 13 June in Macclesfield. The delay was caused by the hospital being slow in getting together various pieces of information. There were a couple of journalists, Ian's parents, the remaining band members except for Bernard, two police officers, my family and myself. I had already met with the coroner and explained the various self-inflicted weals on Ian's body, but was surprised to be questioned on the amount of whisky in the house at the time of Ian's death. I held up my fingers to reveal less than half an inch. My father had the indignity of having to stand up and say he didn't know Ian particularly well. Anyone who had known them both would be well aware that they had only myself in common. Pete Hook remembers my father saying that Ian was 'on another plane':

> 'He wasn't on any plane. He *should* have been on a bleeding plane, the bastard. It's just really sad. I still feel angry to this day; because the whole thing that he wanted, the whole thing that he groomed you for, was success.'
>
> Peter Hook

I felt Rob Gretton expected some kind of concrete conclusion from the inquest; that we would be shown the light and suddenly understand why Ian had done what he did. However, the cause of death was recorded as: 'a. Asphyxia b. Ligature around the neck. The deceased killed himself.' As we left the court room, Peter Hook squeezed my arm and said he was sorry. This was one of the few expressions of sympathy shown to me by Ian's music-business friends and meant a great deal.

As far as I know, I was the last person to see or speak to Ian. The affection held for him by everyone who knew him is obvious by the look on their faces when they tell me they still don't understand why he took his life. His death wasn't simple by any means. Hanging himself was only the final act in his plot of self-destruction. Unknown to Joy Division and their crew, he had talked about suicide since his early teens. If I ever mentioned his early yearnings to die young after our marriage, my questions would be met with neither denial nor explanation. Enlisting the loyal help of those around him to cover his affair with a Belgian woman served to distance me further from events and ensured a total breakdown in communication. Ian's stories about how bad our marriage was caused the rest of Joy Division to underestimate grossly the depth of our relationship. Also, maligning my character would have provided Ian with the means to justify his affair to himself and for a short time allay the guilt he would ultimately feel.

> 'There are different kinds of suicide … I think Ian's was altruistic. He went through some kind of noble gesture. He was completely tormented by himself. He wasn't a businessman; he wasn't someone who could organize it, or arrange it either physically or in his head. I can. I've had affairs, I've been in love with two people at the same time. It's tough because I would use the same intellect that I would use to run Factory, or whatever.'
>
> Tony Wilson

In retrospect we should have all sat around a table in Ian's absence and compared notes. I'm sure we would have realized how much he needed help. Annik's tenacity was astounding – she continued to ring our number long after Ian was dead. The fatal combination of such a lover and a mentor who, on his own admission, could not only justify infidelity but also organize it, compounded Ian's confusion. It would seem that Ian's earlier view on life after the age of twenty-five never really changed. All he needed was the excuse to follow his idols into immortality and being part of Joy Division gave him the tools to build the heart-rending reasons.

Ian's pale blue-green eyes linger on in our daughter and when those familiar long fingers twine themselves unwittingly into those inherited mannerisms, I remember how warm and loved I felt when he and I were sixteen.

'Love Will Tear Us Apart'/'These Days' was released in June 1980 amid jokes about Factory's five-year plan. The powers that be were still unaware that they had been part of Ian's own plan. While some people worried about the myth Tony Wilson was trying to create, no one realized that Ian had been busy myth-making himself. Ian crooned his way through 'Love Will Tear Us Apart' after Tony Wilson gave him Frank Sinatra's *Forty Great Songs* to listen to. When the band were unable to decide which vocal should be used they released both – one on each side of the seven-inch single.

Understandably, the lyrics were interpreted by the press as being about a love affair gone wrong, but as the last to know that our love affair had 'gone wrong', I had taken Ian's infidelity as being part of his illness. Although I hadn't heard the lyrical content, Ian did go to great lengths to explain to me the process by which the image on the sleeve was achieved. The words were etched on a sheet of metal which was then weathered with acid before being left out in the elements. Ian told me that the effect would be to make the metal look like a piece of stone. However, I didn't comprehend that the result would be something resembling a grave stone. His insistence on explaining all this at a time when he could hardly be bothered to look at me makes me think that he was already well ahead with his plans for his demise. I remember being amused by his assumption that I could possibly be interested in a band that I was no longer allowed to see or hear.

Rob Gretton was stunned when I told him the wording I had chosen for the stone in the crematorium, but there seemed little point in changing it as it seemed to encapsulate all I wanted it to say. 'Love will tear us apart' was pretty well how we all felt. The single reached No. 13 in the national chart, but an ongoing union dispute meant that the video was not shown on *Top of the Pops*.

The release of *Closer* brought with it a burst of realization for many of those already close to Ian. His intentions and feelings were all there within the lyrics. While he lived they were equivocal, but with hindsight all was disclosed when it was too late for anything to be done. Such a sensitive composition could not have happened by accident. For me, *Closer* was Ian's valediction and Joy Division's finest work.

He cajoled us, nurtured us with his promises of success. After showing us what it looked like, he offered us a mere sip before he abandoned us on the precipice.

> 'Basically, we want to play and enjoy what we like playing. I think when we stop doing that, I think, well, that will be time to pack it in. That will be the end.'
>
> Ian Curtis, Radio Lancashire interview, 1979

DISCOGRAPHY

Short Circuit 'Live At the Electric Circus' Virgin (VCL 5003), ten-inch album with a special limited-edition pressing on blue vinyl, recorded live during the so-called last two days at the Electric Circus, released June 1978. Joy Division were still called Warsaw at the time of recording and had one track, 'At a Later Date', on the album, as did the Drones, Steel Pulse and the Buzzcocks. The Fall and John Cooper Clarke each had two tracks.

An Ideal for Living Enigma (PSS139), seven-inch four-track EP, recorded at the Pennine Sound Studio, Oldham, December 1977, but not officially released until June 1978: 'Warsaw'/'No Love Lost'/'Leaders of Men'/ 'Failures'.

An Ideal for Living Anonymous Records (ANON 1), twelve-inch version, released September 1978.

A Factory Sample Factory (FAC 2) double EP, recorded at Cargo Studios, Rochdale, 11 October 1978, released January 1979. The Joy Division tracks were 'Digital' and 'Glass', produced by Martin 'Zero' Hannett. Other tracks were by the Durutti Column, John Dowie and Cabaret Voltaire.

The Factory Flick Factory (FAC 9), 8mm film which included 'No City Fun Music', a twelve-minute piece by Joy Division based on an article on *City Fun* magazine by Liz Naylor. It was shown at the Scala Cinema, London, in September 1979.

Unknown Pleasures Factory (FAC 10), debut album, rcorded at Strawberry Studios, Stockport, April 1979, produced by Martin Hannett, released June 1979: 'Inside' had 'She's Lost Control'/'Shadowplay'/ 'Wilderness'/'Interzone'/'I Remember Nothing'; 'Outside' had 'Disorder'/'Day of the Lords'/'Candidate'/'Insight'/'New Dawn Fades'.

Transmission Factory (FAC 13), seven-inch single, recorded at Strawberry Studios, Stockport, July 1979, produced by Martin Hannett, released October 1979; 'Transmission'/'Novelty'.

Earcom 2 Fast (FAST 9), twelve-inch EP, recorded during *Unknown Pleasures* session at Strawberry Studios, Stockport, April 1979, produced by Martin Hannett, given to Edinburgh's Fast label: 'Auto-suggestion'/ 'From Safety to Where . . . ?' Included tracks by Thursdays and Basczax.

Sordide Sentimentale Sordide Sentimentale (SS 33002), 'Atmosphere'/ 'Dead Souls' had been recorded with 'Transmission' and the two songs, both produced by Martin Hannett, were later released in March 1980. Pressed as a limited edition of 1,578 on *Sordide Sentimentale*, it was for sale in France only. The reason for this limited pressing was not apparent from the packaging, but the extravagant three-page sleeve had a text written by Jean-Pierre Turmel, a grim painting by Jean-François Jamoul and a photograph of Joy Division by Anton Corbijn.

Love Will Tear Us Apart Factory (FAC 23), seven-inch single, recorded at Britannia Row Studios, London, March 1980, produced by Martin Hannett, released June 1980, reached No. 13 in UK chart: 'Love Will Tear Us Apart'/'These Days'.

Closer Factory (FAC 25), album, recorded at Britannia Row Studios, London, March 1980, produced by Martin Hannett, released July 1980: 'Atrocity Exhibition'/'Isolation'/'Passover'/'Colony'/'A Means to an End'/'Heart and Soul'/'Twenty Four Hours'/'The Eternal'/'Decades'.

Komakino/Incubation Factory (FAC 28), free flexidisc which also includes uncredited 'As You Said'. 'Komakino' and 'Incubation' were recorded at the same time as *Closer* and appear on the Britannia Row cassette that Ian took home with him after the session.

Atmosphere/She's Lost Control Factory (FACUS 2), twelve-inch single, US release, September 1980 (later to be released in the UK).

Transmission/Novelty Factory (FAC 13), twelve-inch single, remixed US release, September 1980.

Ceremony/In a Lonely Place Factory (FAC 33), two songs written by Joy Division but released in January 1981 by New Order.

Still Factory (FACT 40), double album of studio and live material using tracks from the whole of Joy Division's career, released August 1981: 'Exercise One'/'Ice Age'/'The Sound of Music'/'Glass'/'The Only Mistake'/'Walked In line'/'The Kill'/'Something Must Break'/'Dead Souls'/'Sister Ray'/'Ceremony'/'Shadowplay'/'Means to an End'/ 'Passover'/'New Dawn Fades'/'Transmission'/'Disorder'/'Isolation'/ 'Decades'/'Digital'. Available in standard grey cover or as a deluxe package in a stiff, grey hessian folder with a white ribbon.

Here Are the Young Men Factory (FACT 37), Joy Division video, released August 1982: 'Dead Souls'/'Love Will Tear Us Apart'/'Shadow-play'/'Day of the Lords'/'Digital'/'Colony'/'New Dawn Fades'/'Auto-suggestion'/'Transmission'/'The Sound of Music'/'She's Lost Control'/ 'They Walked In Line'/'I Remember Nothing'.

Atmosphere Factory (FAC 213), UK release, 1988: 'Atmosphere'/'The Only Mistake'/'The Sound of Music'/'Love Will Tear Us Apart'.

Substance Factory (FAC 250), Joy Division compilation album, released in July 1988: 'Warsaw'/'Leaders of Men'/'Digital'/'Auto-suggestion'/ 'Transmission'/'She's Lost Control'/'Incubation'/'Dead Souls'/'Atmo-sphere'/'Love Will Tear Us Apart'/'No Love Lost'/'Failures'/'Glass'/ 'From Safety to Where . . . ?'/'Novelty'/'Komakino'/'These Days'.

Strange Fruit Strange Fruit Records (SFRMC 111), both the Joy Division Peel Sessions, first transmitted in February and December 1979: 'Exercise One'/'Insight'/'She's Lost Control'/'Transmission'/'Love Will Tear Us Apart'/'Twenty-Four Hours'/'Colony'/'The Sound of Music'.

Martin Factory (FACD 325), album that celebrates the work of record producer Martin Hannett, released in 1991 after his death and featuring Joy Division's 'She's Lost Control' with further tracks from the Buzzcocks, Slaughter and the Dogs, John Cooper Clarke, Jilted John, A Certain Ratio, Orchestral Manoeuvres in the Dark, U2, New Order, Happy Mondays, World of Twist, New Fast Automatic Daffodils and the High.

Palatine Factory (FACT 400), a boxed set of four CD albums that tell 'the Factory Story':

Tears in their Eyes (FACD 314) has Joy Division's 'Transmission' and New Order's rendition of 'Ceremony', along with tracks by Orchestral Manoeuvres in the Dark, A Certain Ratio, the Durutti Column, X-O-Dus, ESG, James, Section 25, Stockholm Monsters, Quando Quango.

Life's a Beach (FACD 324) contains tracks from New Order, A Certain Ratio, Section 25, Kalima, Marcel King, Cabaret Voltaire, 52nd Street, Fadela, Quando Quango, Happy Mondays.

The Beat Groups (FACD 334) offers Joy Division's 'Wilderness' with further tracks from Tunnelvision, the Distractions, the Wake, Stockholm Monsters, Happy Mondays, New Order, the Railway Children, the Durutti Column, Miaow, Revenge and James.

Selling Out (FACD 344), appropriately entitled, features Joy Division's 'Atmosphere' with tracks from New Order, Happy Mondays, Northside, the Durutti Column, Steve Martland, Electronic, the Wendys and Cath Carroll.

Permanent: Joy Division, 1995 – Some containing limited edition numbered print – blurred picture of a man sitting with his hand on arm of chair holding a cigarette in right hand – taken from rear right – can't see his face. Photographic images by John Holden, images from the book *Interference*.
Side A: 'Love Will Tear Us Apart'/'Transmission'/'She's Lost Control'/'Shadow Play'. Side B: 'Day of the Lords'/'Isolation'/'Passover'/'Heart and Soul'. Side C: 'Twenty-four Hours'/'These Days'/'Novelty'/'Dead Souls'. Side D: 'The Only Mistake'/'Something Must Break'/'Atmosphere'/'Love Will Tear Us Apart' – Permanent mix (additional production and remix by Don Gehman).

Love Will Tear Us Apart: Joy Division, 1995 – Exclusive mixes by Don Gehman and Arthur Baker. 1, Original version; 2, Radio version (mixed by Don Gehman); 3, Arthur Baker remix (additional production and remix by Arthur Baker); 4, Atmosphere (original Hannett 12"). Remix engineer Mark Plati at Shakedown studios. Photographic images by John Holden, images from the book *Interference*.

Heart and Soul, 1997. Box Set of four CDs:
CD1: **The Kill.** 'Digital'/'Glass'/'Disorder'/'Day of the Lords'/

'Candidate'/'Insight'/'New Dawn Fades'/'She's Lost Control'/
'Shadowplay'/'Wilderness'/'Interzone'/'I Remember Nothing'/'Exer-
cise One'/'Transmission'/'Novelty'/'Auto-suggestion'/ 'From Safety to
Where . . . ?'/'Ice Age'/'The Only Mistake'/'Something Must Break'.
CD2: **She's Lost Control** (12"). 'Atmosphere'/'Dead Souls'/'Love Will
Tear Us Apart'/'These Days'/'The Sound of Music'/'Atrocity Exhi-
bition'/'Isolation'/'Passover'/'Colony'/'A Means to an End'/ 'Heart
and Soul'/'Twenty-four Hours'/'The Eternal'/'Decades'/'Komakino'.
CD3: **Warsaw.** 'No Love Lost'/'Leaders of Men'/'Failures'/'Shadow-
play'/'The Drawback'/'They Walked in Line'/'Glass'/'Candidate'/
'Insight'/'Interzone'/'These Days'/'Colony'/'Ceremony'/'Exercise One'/
'Ice Age'/'The Only Mistake'/'Transmission'/'Something Must Break'/
'Atmosphere'/'Dead Souls'/'Love Will Tear Us Apart'/'In a Lonely
Place'.
CD4: **Disorder.** 'Candidate'/'Insight'/'She's Lost Control'/'These
Days'/'Atrocity Exhibition'/'Isolation'/'Colony'/'The Only Mistake'/
'Wilderness'/'Interzone'/'Novelty'/'Autosuggestion'/'I Remember No-
thing'/'Heart and Soul'/'The Eternal'.

Two young to know, too wild to care . . . 1978–1992. The Factory Story,
Part One. Features Joy Division's 'New Dawn Fades'. London records
(released 1997).

Different colours, different shades . . . 1978–1992. The Factory Story,
Part Two. Features Joy Division's Decades. London records, FACT 2.40
(released 1997).

And here is the young man. Martin Hannett productions, 1978–1991.
Features Joy Division's 'She's Lost Control'. Debutante, PolyGram
(released 1998).

Preston 28 February 1980. 'Incubation'/'Wilderness'/'Twenty-four
Hours'/'The Eternal'/'Heart and Soul'/'Shadowplay'/'Transmission'/
'Disorder'/'Warsaw'/'Colony'/'Interzone'/'She's Lost Control'. Live
album of Preston gig, FACD 2.60 (released 1999).

Warsaw (1977)

3, 5, 0, 1, 2, 5, Go!

I was there in the back stage,
When first light came around.
I grew up like a changeling,
To win the first time around.
I can see all the weakness.
I can pick all the faults.
Well I concede all the faith tests,
Just to stick in your throats.

31G, 31G, 31G

I hung around in your soundtrack,
To mirror all that you've done,
To find the right side of reason,
To kill the three lies for one,
I can see all the cold facts.
I can see through your eyes.
All this talk made no contact.
No matter how hard we tried.

31G, 31G, 31G

I can still hear the footsteps.
I can see only walls.
I slid into your man-traps,
With no hearing at all.
I just see contradiction,
Had to give up the fight,
Just to live in the past tense,
To make believe you were right.

31G, 31G, 31G

3, 5, 0, 1, 2, 5.

Leaders of Men (1977)

Born from some mother's womb,
Just like any other room.
Made a promise for a new life.
Made a victim out of your life.

When your time's on the door,
And it drips to the floor,
And you feel you can touch,
All the noise is too much,
And the seeds that are sown,
Are no longer your own.

Just a minor operation,
To force a final ultimatum.
Thousand words are spoken loud,
Reach the dumb to fool the crowd.

When you walk down the street,
And the sound's not so sweet,
And you wish you could hide,

146

Maybe go for a ride,
To some peep show arcade,
Where the future's not made.

A nightmare situation,
Infiltrate imagination,
Smacks of past Holy wars,
By the wall with broken laws.

The leaders of men,
Born out of your frustration.
The leaders of men,
Just a strange infatuation.
The leaders of men,
Made a promise for a new life.
No saviour for our sakes,
To twist the internees of hate,
Self induced manipulation,
To crush all thoughts of mass salvation.

No Love Lost (1977)

So long sitting here,
Didn't hear the warning.
Waiting for the tape to run.
We've been moving around in different situations,
Knowing that the time would come.
Just to see you torn apart,
Witness to your empty heart.
I need it.
I need it.
I need it.

Through the wire screen, the eyes of those standing outside looked in at her as into the cage of some rare creature in a zoo.

In the hand of one of the assistants she saw the same instrument which they had that morning inserted deep into her body. She shuddered instinctively. No life at all in the house of dolls.

No love lost. No love lost.

You've been seeing things,
In darkness, not in learning,
Hoping that the truth will pass.
No life underground, wasting never changing,
Wishing that this day won't last.
To never see you show your age,
To watch until the beauty fades,
I need it.
I need it.
I need it.

(Second verse on Warsaw album)
Two-way mirror in the hall,
They like to watch everything you do,
Transmitters hidden in the walls,
So they know everything you say is true,
Turn it on,
Don't turn it on,
Turn it on.

Failures (1977)

Don't speak of safe Messiahs,
A failure of the Modern Man,
To the centre of all life's desires,
As a whole not an also ran.
Love in a hollow field,
Break the image of your father's son,

148

Drawn to an inner feel,
He was thought of as the only one,
He was thought of as the only one.

He no longer denies,
All the failures of the Modern Man.
No, no, no, he can't pick sides,
Sees the failures of the Modern Man.
Wise words and sympathy,
Tell the story of our history.
New strength gives a real touch,
Sense and reason make it all too much.
With a strange fatality,
Broke the spirits of a lesser man,
Some other race can see,
In his way he was the only one,
In his way he was the only one.

He no longer denies
All the failures of the Modern Man.
No, no, no, he can't pick sides,
Sees the failures of the Modern Man.
Now that it's right to decide,
In his time he was a total man,
Taken from Caesar's side,
Kept in silence just to prove who's wrong.
He no longer denies,
All the failures of the Modern Man.
No, no, no, he can't pick sides,
Sees the failures of the Modern Man,
All the failures of the Modern Man.

(Waiting for) The Ice Age (1977)
(The first set of lyrics for Ice Age)

Scratching out atrocity,
Splintered in the sand,
In a deathshroud looking back,
Walking hand in hand.
Draw the lines onto your face,
To make it look brand new,
Nothing here will fit in place,
To screen the likes of you.

Stranded in hostility,
Buried further down,
Waiting in a churchyard,
For the sons to come around,
Burning down conventions now,
To give me all the proof,
Nothing here will hold somehow,
To give a glimpse of truth.

Searching for some other life,
To hide behind your door,
On a strange wave plunging down,
With hopes for little more,
Someone might have changed somewhere,
To bring us into line,
All so near to hit and run,
To cut the gaps in time.

Waiting for the cold to come,
To face one final stand,
Viewing scenes in black and white,
Walking hand in hand,

Reaching from the distance,
To find some strength again.

Ice Age (1977)

I've seen the real atrocities,
Buried in the sand,
Stockpiled safety for a few,
While we stand holding hands.

I'm living in the Ice age,
I'm living in the Ice age,
Nothing will hold,
Nothing will fit,
Into the cold,
It's not an eclipse.
Living in the Ice age,
Living in the Ice age,
Living in the Ice age.

Searching for another way,
Hide behind the door,
We'll live in holes and disused shafts,
Hopes for little more.

I'm living in the Ice age,
I'm living in the Ice age,
Nothing will hold,
Nothing will fit,
Into the cold,
No smile on your lips,
Living in the Ice age,
Living in the Ice age,
Living in the Ice age.

Living in the Ice age,
Living in the Ice age,
Living in the Ice age,
Living in the Ice age.

The Kill (1977)

Moved in a hired car,
And I find no way to run,
Adds every moment longer,
Had no time for fun,
Just something that I knew I had to do,
But through it all I left my eyes on you.

I had an impulse to clear it all away,
Oh I used the tactics, make everybody pay,
Just something that I knew I had to do,
But through it all I kept my eyes on you.

Oh, I keep it all clean,
I've paid the graces there,
No kings of misuse,
No sellers of flesh,
Just something that I knew I had to do,
But through it all I kept my eyes on you,
Yeah through it all I kept my eyes on you,
But through it all I kept my eyes on you.

Walked in Line (1978)

All dressed in uniforms so fine,
They drank and killed to pass the time,
Wearing the shame of all their crimes,
With measured steps, they walked in line.

They walked in line,
They walked in line,
They walked in line,
They walked in line,
They walked in line,
They walked in line,
They walked in line,
They walked in line.

They carried pictures of their wives,
And numbered tags to prove their lives,
They walked in line,
They walked in line,
They walked in line,
They walked in line,
They walked in line,
They walked in line,
They walked in line.

Full of a glory never seen,
They made it through the whole machine,
To never question anymore,
Hypnotic trance, they never saw,
They walked in line,
They walked in line,
They walked in line,
They walked in line,
They walked in line,
They walked in line,
They walked in line,
They walked in line,

They walked in line,
They walked in line,

They walked in line,
They walked in line,
They walked in line,
They walked in line,
They walked in line,
They walked in line,
They walked in line,
They walked in line,
They walked in line,
They walked in line,
They walked in line,
They walked in line,
They walked in line,
They walked in line,
Walked in line,
Walked in line.

Exercise One (1978)

When you're looking at life,
In a strange new room,
Maybe drowning soon,
Is this the start of it all?
Turn on your TV,
Turn down your pulse,
Turn away from it all,
It's all getting too much.

When you're looking at life,
Deciphering scars,
Just who fooled who,
Sit still in their cars,
The lights look bright,
When you reach outside,
Time for one last ride,

Before the end of it all.

Digital (1978)

Feel it closing in,
Feel it closing in,
The fear of whom I call,
Every time I call
I feel it closing in,
I feel it closing in,
Day in, day out,
Day in, day out,
Day in, day out,
Day in, day out,
Day in, day out,
Day in, day out.

I feel it closing in,
As patterns seem to form.
I feel it cold and warm.
The shadows start to fall.
I feel it closing in,
I feel it closing in,
Day in, day out,
Day in, day out,
Day in, day out,
Day in, day out,
Day in, day out.

I 'd have the world around,
To see just whatever happens,
Stood by the door alone,
And then it's fade away.
I see you fade away.
Don't ever fade away.

155

I need you here today.
Don't ever fade away.
Don't ever fade away.
Don't ever fade away.
Don't ever fade away.
Fade away. Fade away.
Fade away. Fade away.
Fade away. Fade away.
Fade away.

Glass (1978)

Hearts fail, young hearts fail,
Any time, pressurised,
overheat, overtired.
Take it quick, take it neat,
Clasp your hands, touch your feet.
Take it quick, take it neat,
Take it quick, take it neat.

Hearts fail, young hearts fail,
Anytime, wearing down,
On the run, underground,
Put your hand where it's safe,
Leave your hand where it's safe.

Do it again,
Do it again and again and again.
Do it again and again and again.
Do it again and again and again.
Do it again and again and again.

Anytime, that's your right.
Don't you wish you do it again,
Overheat, overtire.

Don't you wish you do it again,
Don't you wish you do it again,
Don't you wish you do it again,
Any time that's your right,
Don't you wish you do it again,
Any time that's your right.
Don't you wish you do it again,
Don't you wish you do it again,
I bet you wish you do it again.
Do it again.
Do it again.
Do it again.

Disorder (1979)

I've been waiting for a guide to come and take me by the hand,
Could these sensations make me feel the pleasures of a normal man?
These sensations barely interest me for another day,
I've got the spirit, lose the feeling, take the shock away.

It's getting faster, moving faster now, it's getting out of hand,
On the tenth floor, down the back stairs, it's a no man's land,
Lights are flashing, cars are crashing, getting frequent now ,
I've got the spirit, lose the feeling, let it out somehow.

What means to you, what means to me, and we will meet again,
I'm watching you, I'm watching her, I'll take no pity from your
friends,
Who is right, who can tell, and who gives a damn right now,
Until the spirit new sensation takes hold, then you know,
Until the spirit new sensation takes hold, then you know,
Until the spirit new sensation takes hold, then you know.
I've got the spirit, but lose the feeling,
I've got the spirit, but lose the feeling.
Feeling, feeling, feeling, feeling, feeling, feeling, feeling.

Day of the Lords (1979)

This is the room, the start of it all,
No portrait so fine, only sheets on the wall,
I've seen the nights, filled with bloodsport and pain,
And the bodies obtained, the bodies obtained.

Where will it end? Where will it end?
Where will it end? Where will it end?

These are your friends from childhood, through youth,
Who goaded you on, demanded more proof,
Withdrawal pain is hard, it can do you right in,
So distorted and thin, distorted and thin.

Where will it end? Where will it end?
Where will it end? Where will it end?

This is the car at the edge of the road,
There's nothing disturbed, all the windows are closed,
I guess you were right, when we talked in the heat,
There's no room for the weak, no room for the weak,

Where will it end? Where will it end?
Where will it end? Where will it end?

This is the room, the start of it all,
Through childhood, through youth, I remember it all,
Oh, I've seen the nights filled with bloodsport and pain.
And the bodies obtained, the bodies obtained, the bodies obtained.

Where will it end? Where will it end?
Where will it end? Where will it end?

Candidate (1979)

Forced by the pressure,
The territories marked,
No longer the pleasure,
Oh, I've since lost the heart.

Corrupted from memory,
No longer the power,
It's creeping up slowly,
That last fatal hour.

Oh, I don't know what made me,
What gave me the right,
To mess with your values,
And change wrong to right.

Please keep your distance,
The trail leads to here,
There's blood on your fingers,
Brought on by fear.

I campaigned for nothing,
I worked hard for this,
I tried to get to you,
You treat me like this.

It's just second nature,
It's what we've been shown,
We're living by your rules,
That's all that we know.

I tried to get to you,
I tried to get to you,
I tried to get to you.

I tried to get to you.

Insight (1979)

Guess your dreams always end.
They don't rise up just descend,
But I don't care anymore,
I've lost the will to want more,
I'm not afraid not at all,
I watch them all as they fall,
But I remember when we were young.

Those with habits of waste,
Their sense of style and good taste,
Of making sure you were right,
Hey don't you know you were right?
I'm not afraid anymore,
I keep my eyes on the door,
But I remember ….

Tears of sadness for you,
More upheaval for you,
Reflects a moment in time,
A special moment in time,
Yeah we wasted our time,
We didn't really have time,
But we remember when we were young.

And all God's angels beware,
And all you judges beware,
Sons of chance, take good care,
For all the people not there,
I'm not afraid anymore,
I'm not afraid anymore,
I'm not afraid anymore,

Oh, I'm not afraid anymore.

New Dawn Fades (1979)

A change of speed, a change of style.
A change of scene, with no regrets,
A chance to watch, admire the distance,
Still occupied, though you forget.
Different colours, different shades,
Over each mistakes were made.
I took the blame.
Directionless so plain to see,
A loaded gun won't set you free.
So you say.

We'll share a drink and step outside,
An angry voice and one who cried,
'We'll give you everything and more,
The strain's too much, can't take much more.'
Oh, I've walked on water, run through fire,
Can't seem to feel it anymore.
It was me, waiting for me,
Hoping for something more,
Me, seeing me this time, hoping for something else.

She's Lost Control (1979)

Confusion in her eyes that says it all.
She's lost control.
And she's clinging to the nearest passer by,
She's lost control.
And she gave away the secrets of her past,
And said I've lost control again,
And of a voice that told her when and where to act,
She said I've lost control again.

And she turned around and took me by the hand and said,
I've lost control again.
And how I'll never know just why or understand,
She said I've lost control again.
And she screamed out kicking on her side and said,
I've lost control again.
And seized up on the floor, I thought she'd die.
She said I've lost control.
She's lost control again.
She's lost control.
She's lost control again.
She's lost control.

Well I had to 'phone her friend to state my case,
And say she's lost control again.
And she showed up all the errors and mistakes,
And said I've lost control again.
But she expressed herself in many different ways,
Until she lost control again.
And walked upon the edge of no escape,
And laughed I've lost control.
She's lost control again.
She's lost control.
She's lost control again.
She's lost control.

Shadowplay (1979)

To the centre of the city where all roads meet, waiting for you,
To the depths of the ocean where all hopes sank, searching for you,
I was moving through the silence without motion, waiting for you,
In a room with a window in the corner I found truth.

In the shadowplay, acting out your own death, knowing no more,
As the assassins all grouped in four lines, dancing on the floor,

And with cold steel, odour on their bodies made a move to connect,
But I could only stare in disbelief as the crowds all left.

I did everything, everything I wanted to,
I let them use you for their own ends,
To the centre of the city in the night, waiting for you,
To the centre of the city in the night, waiting for you.

Wilderness (1979)

I travelled far and wide through many different times,
What did you see there?
I saw the saints with their toys,
What did you see there?
I saw all knowledge destroyed.
I travelled far and wide through many different times.

I travelled far and wide through prisons of the cross,
What did you see there?
The power and glory of sin,
What did you see there?
The blood of Christ on their skins,
I travelled far and wide through many different times.

I travelled far and wide and unknown martyrs died,
What did you see there?
I saw the one sided trials,
What did you see there?
I saw the tears as they cried,
They had tears in their eyes,
Tears in their eyes,
Tears in their eyes,
Tears in their eyes.

Interzone (1978)

I walked through the city limits,
Someone talked me in to do it,
Attracted by some force within it,
Had to close my eyes to get close to it,
Around a corner where a prophet lay,
Saw the place where she'd a room to stay,
A wire fence where the children played.
Saw the bed where the body lay,
And I was looking for a friend of mine.
And I had no time to waste.
Yeah, looking for some friends of mine.

The cars screeched hear the sound on dust,
Heard a noise just a car outside,
Metallic blue turned red with rust,
Pulled in close by the building's side,
In a group all forgotten youth,
Had to think, collect my senses now,
Are turned on to a knife edged view.
Find some places where my friends don't know,
And I was looking for a friend of mine,
And had no time to waste.
Yeah, looking for some friends of mine.

Down the dark streets, the houses looked the same,
Getting darker now, faces look the same,
And I walked round and round.
No stomach, torn apart,
Nail me to a train.
Had to think again,
Trying to find a clue, trying to find a way to get out!
Trying to move away, had to move away and keep out.

164

Four, twelve windows, ten in a row,
Behind a wall, well I looked down low,
The lights shined like a neon show,
Inserted deep felt a warmer glow,
No place to stop, no place to go,
No time to lose, had to keep on going,
I guess they died some time ago.
I guess they died some time ago.
And I was looking for a friend of mine
And I had no time to waste.
Yeah, looking for some friends of mine.

I Remember Nothing (1979)

We were strangers.
We were strangers, for way too long, for way too long,
We were strangers, for way too long.
Violent, violent,
Were strangers.

Get weak all the time, may just pass the time,
Me in my own world, yeah you there beside,
The gaps are enormous, we stare from each side,
We were strangers for way too long.

Violent, more violent, his hand cracks the chair,
Moves on reaction, then slumps in despair,
Trapped in a cage and surrendered too soon,
Me in my own world, the one that you knew,
For way too long.
We were strangers for way too long.
We were strangers,
We were strangers for way too long,
For way too long.

Transmission (1978)

Radio, live transmission.
Radio, live transmission.

Listen to the silence, let it ring on.
Eyes, dark grey lenses frightened of the sun.
We would have a fine time living in the night,
Left to blind destruction,
Waiting for our sight.

And we would go on as though nothing was wrong.
And hide from these days we remained all alone.
Staying in the same place, just staying out the time.
Touching from a distance,
Further all the time.

Dance, dance, dance, dance, dance, to the radio.
Dance, dance, dance, dance, dance, to the radio.
Dance, dance, dance, dance, dance, to the radio.
Dance, dance, dance, dance, dance, to the radio.

Well I could call out when the going gets tough.
The things that we've learnt are no longer enough.
No language, just sound, that's all we need know, to synchronise
love to the beat of the show.

And we could dance.

Dance, dance, dance, dance, dance, to the radio.
Dance, dance, dance, dance, dance, to the radio.
Dance, dance, dance, dance, dance, to the radio.
Dance, dance, dance, dance, dance, to the radio.

Autosuggestion (1979)

Here, here,
Everything is by design,
Everything is by design.

Here, here,
Everything is kept inside.
So take a chance and step outside,
Your hopes, your dreams, your paradise.
Heroes, idols cracked like ice.

Here, here,
Everything is kept inside.
So take a chance and step outside.
Pure frustration face to face.
A point of view creates more waves,
So take a chance and step outside.

Take a chance and step outside.
Lose some sleep and say you tried.
Meet frustration face to face.
A point of view creates more waves.

So lose some sleep and say you tried.
So lose some sleep and say you tried.
So lose some sleep and say you tried.
So lose some sleep and say you tried.
Say you tried.
Say you tried.
Say you tried.
Say you tried.
Say you tried.
Say you tried.
Say you tried.

Say you tried.
Say you tried.
Say you tried.
Say you tried.
Yeah, lose some sleep and say you tried.
Yeah, lose some sleep and say you tried.
Yeah, lose some sleep and say you tried.
Yeah, lose some sleep and say you tried.

From Safety to Where … ? (1979)

No I don't know just why.
No I don't know just why.
Which way to turn,
I got this ticket to use.

Through childlike ways rebellion and crime,
To reach this point and retreat back again.
The broken hearts,
All the wheels that have turned,
The memories scarred and the vision is blurred.

No I don't know which way,
Don't know which way to turn,
The best possible use.

Just passing through, 'till we reach the next stage.
But just to where, well it's all been arranged.
Just passing through but the break must be made.
Should we move on or stay safely away?

Through childlike ways rebellion and crime,
To reach this point and retreat back again.
The broken hearts,
All the wheels that have turned,

The memories scarred and the vision is blurred.

Just passing through, 'till we reach the next stage.
But just to where, well it's all been arranged.
Just passing through but the break must be made.
Should we move on or stay safely away?

Atmosphere (1979)

Walk in silence,
Don't walk away, in silence.
See the danger,
Always danger,
Endless talking,
Life rebuilding,
Don't walk away.

Walk in silence,
Don't turn away, in silence.
Your confusion,
My illusion,
Worn like a mask of self-hate,
Confronts and then dies.
Don't walk away.

People like you find it easy,
Naked to see,
Walking on air.
Hunting by the rivers,
Through the streets,
Every corner abandoned too soon,
Set down with due care.
Don't walk away in silence,
Don't walk away.

Dead Souls (1979)

Someone take these dreams away,
That point me to another day,
A duel of personalities,
That stretch all true realities.

That keep calling me,
They keep calling me,
Keep on calling me,
They keep calling me.

Where figures from the past stand tall,
And mocking voices ring the halls.
Imperialistic house of prayer,
Conquistadors who took their share.

That keep calling me,
They keep calling me,
Keep on calling me,
They keep calling me.

Calling me, calling me, calling me, calling me.

They keep calling me,
Keep on calling me,
They keep calling me.
They keep calling me.

Love Will Tear Us Apart (1980)

When routine bites hard,
And ambitions are low,
And resentment rides high,
But emotions won't grow,

And we're changing our ways, taking different roads.

Then love, love will tear us apart again.
Love, love will tear us apart again.

Why is the bedroom so cold?
You've turned away on your side.
Is my timing that flawed?
Our respect runs so dry.
Yet there's still this appeal that we've kept through our lives.

But love, love will tear us apart again.
Love, love will tear us apart again.

You cry out in your sleep,
All my failings exposed.
And there's a taste in my mouth,
As desperation takes hold.
Just that something so good just can't function no more.

But love, love will tear us apart again.
Love, love will tear us apart again.
Love, love will tear us apart again.
Love, love will tear us apart again.

These Days (1980)

Morning seems strange, almost out of place.
Searched hard for you and your special ways.
These days, these days.

Spent all my time, learnt a killer's art.
Took threats and abuse 'till I'd learned the part.
Can you stay for these days?

These days, these days.

Used outward deception to get away,
Broken heart romance to make it pay.

These days, these days.

We'll drift through it all, it's the modern age.
Take care of it all now these debts are paid.
Can you stay for these days?

The Sound of Music (1979)

See my true reflection,
Cut off my own connections,
I can see life getting harder,
So sad is this sensation,
 Reverse the situation,
I can't see it getting better.

I'll walk you through the heartbreak,
Show you all the out takes,
I can't see it getting higher,
Systematically degraded,
Emotionally a scapegoat,
I can't see it getting better.

Perverse and unrealistic,
Try to make it all stick,
I can't see it getting better,
Hollow now, I'm burned out,
All I need to break out,
I can't see life getting higher,
Love, life, makes you feel higher,
Love, of life, makes you feel higher,

Higher, higher, higher, higher,
Higher, higher, higher, higher,
Love of life, makes you feel higher.

The Only Mistake (1979)

Made the fatal mistake,
Like I did once before,
A tendency just to take,
Till the purpose turned sour,

Strain, take the strain, these days we love,
Strain, take the strain, these days we love.

Yeah, the only mistake was that you ran away,
Avenues lined with trees, strangled words for the day,
Yeah, the only mistake, like I made once before,
Yeah, the only mistake, could have made it before.

Strain, take the strain, these days we love,
Strain, take the strain, these days we love.

And the only mistake, led to rumours unfound,
Led to pressures unknown, different feelings and sounds,
Yeah, the only mistake, like I made once before,
Yeah, the only mistake, could have made it before.

Atrocity Exhibition (1980)

Asylums with doors open wide,
Where people had paid to see inside,
For entertainment they watch his body twist,
Behind his eyes he says, 'I still exist.'

This is the way, step inside.

This is the way, step inside.
This is the way, step inside.
This is the way, step inside.

In arenas he kills for a prize,
Wins a minute to add to his life.
But the sickness is drowned by cries for more,
Pray to God, make it quick, watch him fall.

This is the way, step inside.
This is the way, step inside.
This is the way, step inside.
This is the way, step inside.

This is the way.
This is the way.
This is the way.
This is the way.
This is the way, step inside.
This is the way, step inside.
This is the way, step inside.
This is the way, step inside.

You'll see the horrors of a faraway place,
Meet the architects of law face to face.
See mass murder on a scale you've never seen,
And all the ones who try hard to succeed.

This is the way, step inside.
This is the way, step inside.
This is the way, step inside.
This is the way, step inside.

And I picked on the whims of a thousand or more,
Still pursuing the path that's been buried for years,

All the dead wood from jungles and cities on fire,
Can't replace or relate, can't release or repair,
Take my hand and I'll show you what was and will be.

Isolation (1980)

In fear every day, every evening,
He calls her aloud from above,
Carefully watched for a reason,
Painstaking devotion and love,
Surrendered to self preservation,
From others who care for themselves.
A blindness that touches perfection,
But hurts just like anything else.

Isolation, isolation, isolation.

Mother I tried please believe me,
I'm doing the best that I can.
I'm ashamed of the things I've been put through,
I'm ashamed of the person I am.

Isolation, isolation, isolation.

But if you could just see the beauty,
These things I could never describe,
These pleasures a wayward distraction,
This is my one lucky prize.

Isolation, isolation, isolation, isolation, isolation.

Passover (1980)

This is a crisis I knew had to come,
Destroying the balance I'd kept.

Doubting, unsettling and turning around,
Wondering what will come next.
Is this the role that you wanted to live?
I was foolish to ask for so much.
Without the protection and infancy's guard,
It all falls apart at first touch.

Watching the reel as it comes to a close,
Brutally taking its time,
People who change for no reason at all,
It's happening all of the time.
Can I go on with this train of events?
Disturbing and purging my mind,
Back out of my duties, when all's said and done,
I know that I'll lose every time.

Moving along in our God given ways,
Safety is sat by the fire,
Sanctuary from these feverish smiles,
Left with a mark on the door,
Is this the gift that I wanted to give?
Forgive and forget's what they teach,
Or pass through the deserts and wastelands once more,
And watch as they drop by the beach.

This is the crisis I knew had to come,
Destroying the balance I'd kept,
Turning around to the next set of lives,
Wondering what will come next.

Colony (1980)

A cry for help, a hint of anaesthesia,
The sound from broken homes,
We used to always meet here.

As he lays asleep, she takes him in her arms,
Some things I have to do, but I don't mean you harm.

A worried parent's glance, a kiss, a last goodbye,
Hands him the bag she packed, the tears she tries to hide,
A cruel wind that bows down to our lunacy,
And leaves him standing cold here in this colony.

I can't see why all these confrontations,
I can't see why all these dislocations,
No family life, this makes me feel uneasy,
Stood alone here in this colony.
In this colony, in this colony, in this colony, in this colony.

Dear God in his wisdom took you by the hand,
God in his wisdom made you understand.
God in his wisdom took you by the hand,
God in his wisdom made you understand.
God in his wisdom took you by the hand,
God in his wisdom made you understand.
God in his wisdom took you by the hand,
God in his wisdom made you understand.
In this colony, in this colony, in this colony, in this colony.

A Means to an End (1980)

A legacy so far removed,
One day will be improved.
Eternal rights we left behind,
We were the better kind.
Two the same, set free too,
I always looked to you,
I always looked to you,
I always looked to you.

We fought for good, stood side by side,
Our friendship never died.
On stranger waves, the lows and highs,
Our vision touched the sky,
Immortalists with points to prove,
I put my trust in you.
I put my trust in you.
I put my trust in you.

A house somewhere on foreign soil,
Where ageing lovers call,
Is this your goal, your final needs,
Where dogs and vultures eat,
Committed still I turn to go.
I put my trust in you.
I put my trust in you.
I put my trust in you.
I put my trust in you.
In you. In you. In you.
Put my trust in you, in you.

Heart and Soul (1980)

Instincts that can still betray us,
A journey that leads to the sun,
Soulless and bent on destruction,
A struggle between right and wrong.
You take my place in the showdown,
I'll observe with a pitiful eye,
I'd humbly ask for forgiveness,
A request well beyond you and I.

Heart and soul, one will burn.
Heart and soul, one will burn.

An abyss that laughs at creation,
A circus complete with all fools,
Foundations that lasted the ages,
Then ripped apart at their roots.
Beyond all this good is the terror,
The grip of a mercenary hand,
When savagery turns all good reason,
There's no turning back, no last stand.

Heart and soul, one will burn.
Heart and soul, one will burn.

Existence well what does it matter?
I exist on the best terms I can.
The past is now part of my future,
The present is well out of hand.
The present is well out of hand.

Heart and soul, one will burn.
Heart and soul, one will burn.
One will burn, one will burn.
Heart and soul, one will burn.

Twenty-four Hours (1980)

So this is permanence, love's shattered pride.
What once was innocence, turned on its side.
A cloud hangs over me, marks every move,
Deep in the memory, of what once was love.

Oh how I realised how I wanted time,
Put into perspective, tried so hard to find,
Just for one moment, thought I'd found my way.
Destiny unfolded, I watched it slip away.

Excessive flashpoints, beyond all reach,
Solitary demands for all I'd like to keep.
Let's take a ride out, see what we can find,
A valueless collection of hopes and past desires.

I never realised the lengths I'd have to go,
All the darkest corners of a sense I didn't know.
Just for one moment, I heard somebody call,
Looked beyond the day in hand, there's nothing there at all.

Now that I've realised how it's all gone wrong,
Gotta find some therapy, this treatment takes too long.
Deep in the heart of where sympathy held sway,
Gotta find my destiny, before it gets too late.

The Eternal (1980)

Procession moves on, the shouting is over,
Praise to the glory of loved ones now gone.
Talking aloud as they sit round their tables,
Scattering flowers washed down by the rain.
Stood by the gate at the foot of the garden,
Watching them pass like clouds in the sky,
Try to cry out in the heat of the moment,
Possessed by a fury that burns from inside.

Cry like a child, though these years make me older,
With children my time is so wastefully spent,
A burden to keep, though their inner communion,
Accept like a curse an unlucky deal.
Played by the gate at the foot of the garden,
My view stretches out from the fence to the wall,
No words could explain, no actions determine,
Just watching the trees and the leaves as they fall.

Decades (1980)

Here are the young men, the weight on their shoulders,
Here are the young men, well where have they been?
We knocked on the doors of Hell's darker chamber,
Pushed to the limit, we dragged ourselves in,
Watched from the wings as the scenes were replaying,
We saw ourselves now as we never had seen.
Portrayal of the trauma and degeneration,
The sorrows we suffered and never were free.

Where have they been?
Where have they been?
Where have they been?
Where have they been?

Weary inside, now our heart's lost forever,
Can't replace the fear, or the thrill of the chase,
Each ritual showed up the door for our wanderings,
Open then shut, then slammed in our face.

Where have they been?
Where have they been?
Where have they been?
Where have they been?

Komakino (1980)

This is the hour when the mysteries emerge.
A strangeness so hard to reflect.
A moment so moving, goes straight to your heart,
The vision has never been met.
The attraction is held like a weight deep inside,
Something I'll never forget.

The pattern is set, her reaction will start,
Complete but rejected too soon.
Looking ahead in the grip of each fear,
Recalls the life that we knew.
The shadow that stood by the side of the road,
Always reminds me of you.

How can I find the right way to control,
All the conflict inside, all the problems beside,
As the questions arise, and the answers don't fit,
Into my way of things,
Into my way of things.

She's Lost Control (extended version)

Confusion in her eyes that said it all.
She's lost control.
And she's clinging to the nearest passer by,
She's lost control.
And she gave away the secrets of her past,
And said I've lost control again,
And of a voice that told her when and where to act,
She said I've lost control again.

And she turned to me and took me by the hand and said,
I've lost control again.
And how I'll never know just why or understand,
She said I've lost control again.
And she screamed out kicking on her side and said,
I've lost control again.
And seized up on the floor, I thought she'd die.
She said I've lost control again.
She's lost control again.
She's lost control.
She's lost control again.

She's lost control.

Well I had to 'phone her friend to state her case,
And say she's lost control again.
And she showed up all the errors and mistakes.
And said I've lost control again.
But she expressed herself in many different ways,
Until she lost control again.
And walked upon the edge of no escape,
And laughed I've lost control again.
She's lost control again.
She's lost control.
She's lost control again.
She's lost control.

I could live a little better with the myths and the lies,
When the darkness broke in, I just broke down and cried.
I could live a little in a wider line,
When the change is gone, when the urge is gone,
To lose control. When here we come.

Something Must Break (1980)

Two ways to choose,
On a razors edge,
Remain behind,
Go straight ahead.

Room full of people, room for just one,
If I can't break out now, the time just won't come.

Two ways to choose,
Which way to go,
Decide for me,
Please let me know.

Looked in the mirror, saw I was wrong,
If I could get back to where I belong, where I belong.

Two ways to choose,
Which way to go,
Had thoughts for one
Designs for both.

But we were immortal, we were not there,
Washed up on the beaches, struggling for air.

I see your face still in my window,
Torments yet calms, won't set me free,
Something must break now,
This life isn't mine,
Something must break now,
Wait for the time,
Something must break.

Ceremony (1980)

This is why events unnerve me,
They find it all, a different story,
Notice whom for wheels are turning,
Turn again and turn towards this time,
All she ask's the strength to hold me,
Then again the same old story,
Word will travel, oh so quickly,
Travel first and lean towards this time.

Oh, I'll break them down, no mercy shown,
Heaven knows, it's got to be this time,
Watching her, these things she said,
The times she cried,
Too frail to wake this time.

Oh I'll break them down, no mercy shown
Heaven knows, it's got to be this time,
Avenues all lined with trees,
Picture me and then you start watching,
Watching forever, forever,
Watching love grow, forever,
Letting me know, forever.

In a Lonely Place (1980)

Caressing the marble and stone,
Love that was special for one,
The waste in the fever I heat,
How I wish you were here with me now.

Body that curls in and dies,
And shares that awful daylight,
Warm like a dog round your feet,
How I wish you were here with me now.

Hangman looks round as he waits,
Cord stretches tight then it breaks,
Someday we will die in your dreams,
How I wish we were here with you now.

Unfinished Writings

Men who forget,
As empires start to crack,
Men who forget brought up to
Men who just lack,
Any justice and
Any thoughts for
Bitter and torn,
All prejudice for the like,
Turning out one by one,
Clasp your hands, don't forget,
Minority hold.

*

Perverse reactions, the failings of mankind. What is your disability? What cross do you bear? Will your crucifiction leave a better place for your children, your children's children. Can you expect so much as terrors of the modern age loom over distant hills, in violent cities, quiet towns and settled homes. Ignorance, a poor man's friend. Avenues lined with trees and bitter memories. Technology and the ghosts of Christmas past. A family that haunts even in your more friendly dreams, Father can I go out now … Father can I go, Father … Who are you? Where am I? What am I?

*

Nothing seems real anymore. Even the flames from the fire seem to beckon to me, drawing me into some great past life buried somewhere deep in my subconscious, if only I could find the key.. if only.. if only. Ever since my illness, my condition, I've been trying to find some logical way of passing my time, of justifying a means to an end.

*

Someone called her name … Taking her children by the hand she walked over to the other side of the room and glanced sideways out

of the window, straightening the mirror on her way. Nothing.
Someone called her name … Children are crying in their bedrooms.
Don't you know it takes something more to cope with these prob-
lems, this stress. This I can take but the way some people look at me,
the way some people talk, really gets me down. This is all I want.
This is all I came for. This is my life.

Someone called her name. A noise outside breaks the afternoon
silence.
'Aren't you glad I came. I need someone to realise my dreams. I can
take you away from all this. I've already seen your daughter. I
picked her up in my car on her way to school this morning. She's
beautiful. Don't you think you need a change too.'
Someone called her name. Sound of children crying.

*

Cold wind moving in from afar – death in the park, another sense-
less murder, child mutilated, red sky calling, inserts deep inside,
warm glow from the feet up – this could be Hell.

Twelve noon lined up against the wall – about face, load fire. Ten
shots echo in faraway African town. CIA report 'No cause to worry –
everything under control.'

On the beach looking for old friends – cities springing up all around
– metallic glow reflecting a coldness felt only once in childhood.
Money for this, money for that, money for nothing. I guess they died
some time ago. Walking on water – Moses crosses the Red Sea –
world peace intact, with a deep sigh he turns to face the wall, hand
in hand they disappear into the night.

*

Pictures, brown round the edges, occupying places on half empty
walls. As the dust gathers so do the memories of a child's past.
Healing wounds opened again and letters in strictest confidence for

the world to see. Follow me down the garden path, I'll show you where it all happened, oh so many years ago. Follow me down the path. Tears of a brother lost before birth, sentenced to no life at all. Tears of a mother who knew she had lost everything.

'We left her playing here beside the flowers and then ... It was horrible. I just can't bear to think about it.'

The clock strikes six, everyone eats and then sleeps. A deep uneasy sleep. I can't understand why. Pacing the floor, I stare out into the night. What's left for me?

*

A wider alliance that leads to new roads beyond the limits, holding hands, jumping off walls into dark seclusion, cut off from the mainstream of most intimate yearnings, I left my heart somewhere on the other side, I left all desire for good.

Clinging to naked thought, impossible tactics worked out for impossible means. This is the final moment of respite. The final page in the book. A bitter challenge between old and new, with one last warning.

Out of Touch (1977)

On the wasteline,
Heartbreak, mainline,
In a hurry to get somewhere.
Divorced from what's real so early.
All a waste of nothing really.
Arrive too late – don't you know you're out of touch?

Pass the dateline,
All on your time.
In a hurry to get something.
Staring at your own two faces,
Feeding off your private crazes.
You're out on you're own – out – out of touch.

Nervous feeling,
No scene stealing,
Can you reach the outer limits?
Stuck inside your pen too long,
Forgotten moves where you went wrong.
You've lost the feeling, now you're out of touch.

Empty station,
Too long waiting,
In a hurry to get somewhere,
 Divorced from everything so early,

All a waste of nothing really,
You were never there always out of touch.

Deadline (1979)

Destinations always change,
It could be hours,
It seems like days,
Wait around as though nothing's wrong,
But heaven knows we've tried so long,
To do the final breakthrough.

A choice of gifts,
With cards to deal,
A narrow table,
Legs of steel,
A window seat with views the same,
All down the line we play the game,
For two, now we are two.

Destinations never change,
It seems as though we're days away,
And all the points that lead us to,
We never stop, just pass on thru' again,
Do it again.

Driftwood (1979)

Moving on out in a new line,
Setting our course by the sun,
Leaving the shoreline behind us,
We're drifting apart while we run.

Wheels are in motion above us,
Metal and power in disguise,

Scared of the danger around us,
We're drowning in our paradise.

Wreckage and gold on the sea bed,
Souls we could never reclaim,
Grey are the skies that surround us,
Forcing us farther away.

Moving on out in a new line,
Setting our course by the sun,
Leaving it all way behind us,
We're drifting apart as we run.

Conditioned
(an unrecorded early Warsaw song. Some of the lyrics were later reworked for Exercise One)

Sure I'll see you drown,
You do for me, I did for you,
You're on the rim of wheels that turn
In ignorance, no way to learn.

Cure just takes you down,
Not down for good, that's understood,
Lights on green, borrowed times,
It's just the same, a different name.

Conditioned – you,
Conditioned – me,
No way out that I can see,
Conditioned – you,
Conditioned – me,
Who selects your destiny?

Just who's in the chair,

To think for me to make me care –
Turn down the TV,
Turn down my pulse,
Control my heart,
The sound's too much.

Untitled

Just watchin' you –
Tearing strips off just for fun to get a better fit.
All eyes on you – sex induced, the labour proves,
Just watching every drip,
Waiting for you – bought us out to close all doors with broken laws
– your laws don't fit.

It's all so coldly logical without a trace of fear,
Intentions, mask indifference, built up throughout the years.
Not televised, conceals the motives,
Not waiting for ease,
Till the cancer grows,
Replacing hope and you are the disease.

Just watchin' you –
Some minor incident –
An instant eyes turn blind,
All eyes in you –
Just some kind of accident,
In God's name, left behind,
Waiting for you –
Detroying gains,
All lost in vain, but kept in mind – you're way behind.

Some stranger atrocity commit in silence now,
Not in these times, another world, but it's so close somehow,
A shattered nerve, for those who serve, the reason lost its way.

In streets of fear and all those here, the internees of hate.

Just watchin' you – tearing strips off just for fun to get a better fit,
All eyes on you – broken causes, no one knows the real cause, you're it.
Waiting for you – ultimatum, change it soon don't cling to every bit
– it just won't fit.

Secret (1978)

He desires love, in some special way,
Against all perversion,
Fed with fruits of decay.
He remembers,
How the guilty have seen,
All the pure but selfish,
Buried deep in his dreams.

He sees a vision in the sky,
Looking down at him,
Calling him by name.
Yeah he sees faces from yesterday,
Of what might have been,
But the past must still remain.

He desires love,
Not some perfect affair,
In hotels of steel and glass,
Just to cross on the stairs,
But he can still see,
All the angels in time,
As his dreams of ecstasy,
Turned to nightmares of crime.

He sees a vision in the sky,

Looking down at him,
How the past will still remain.
Yeah he sees a vision in the sky,
Staring down at him,
He'll always see the same.

Sure I'll see you down,
You do for me I did for you,
Cure just takes you down,
We're down for good that's understood.

Untitled (1978)

I can see a thousand wills just bending in the night.
And all the pretty faces painted grey to match the sky,
From a distance seeing friends just washed up on the shore,
A picture in my mind of what's to come before the storm.

In time, we don't belong in our own lifetime.

I can hear the voices lost in echoes as they build,
New homes to hide the sadness that the search for more had killed,
From a by road seeing friends just washed up on the shore.
Picture in my mind of what's to come before the storm.

In time, we don't belong in our own lifetime.

I can feel an emptiness and see heads held in shame,
Trapped inside a legacy of everyone to blame.
In the distance see myself just washed up on the shore,
A picture in my mind of what will come before the storm.

In time, we don't belong to our own lifetime.

We won't crawl and never show our faces,

We'll stand firm and never show the traces,
Of the fear we knew but always could disguise,
Of this sinking feeling hid behind our eyes.

Untitled

In the back of my mind,
All I feel is mistrust,
In the back of my mind,
All I see is the dirt,
Segregation of thoughts,
Ideals turning to dust.

Where some houses once stood,
Stands a man with a gun,
In some neighbourhood,
A father hangs up his son,
In the back of my mind.

Untitled

Don't think I'd have stayed just for one more day,
It seems so much like home,
No room to go astray,
Don't think I could watch – with
mindless, empty tasks,
Intake moving in, forced to walk a lonely path.

Pictures all around, of how good a life should be,
A model for the rest,
That bred insecurity,
I walked a jagged line and then came back for more,
It's always in my mind,
An institution with no law.

Day of the Lords (1978)

We won't forget you on the day of the lords,
When our hearts stopped,
When we put up the boards,
To relax from all this sickness of words,
To escape from the collapse of our worlds.

We won't forget you, though in violence you go,
As the wheels turned in the theatres below,
An escape from the ends never met,
In apartments with the lives not formed yet.

You never really understood,
You never tried to change our minds,
As long as you were in control,
As long as we could spare the time,
And 'cause you needed to win on the day of the lords.

We won't forget you on the day of the lords,
In a new town, just clutching at straws,
With the door shut, now the running has ended,
And a last thought of the chances surrrendered.

End of Time (1978)

We resist all of times mutations,
And lose our hands for all lost creations,
We left holes in the best laid plans,
And registered every inward glance.

For all mysteries never seen and never revealed,
And the memories, always tired and never too real,
Yeah, the memories, down on paper cease to exist,
To uncover all true feelings inside just too much to risk.

We made out down the roads to nowhere,
And lost all purpose in the rush to get there,
From broken homes built on dust and ashes,
That marked the spots of last years crashes.

For all mysteries never seen and never revealed,
And the memories, always hazy, never too real,
Yeah, the memories of a future everyone shared,
But when the time came, looking over our shoulders,
Nobody cared.

Untitled (1978)

I walked out and I thought for a time I could see
No defence, and I thought for a while you were me,
We were wrong,
In our time,
Always down,
Out of line.

I relaxed from the days filled with blood sport in vain,
And returned with the knowledge that we're two the same,
Two in Hell,
Two set free,
Too alike,
You to me.

And we watched everything pass us by in due course,
Always tied by a mutual feeling that lost,
We were two,
Two in Hell,
Two set free,
Known too well.

Untitled (1978)

Searching for some other way,
To bring some small relief,
Never to be satisfied,
And snatch at all beliefs.

Didn't have the energy,
To make up for my part,
Everything seemed easy but
I didn't have the heart.

Things that on the surface,
Seemed so very much the same,
But once you've made the move,
So long nothing else remains.

So afraid to make a break,
For fear of what I'd do,
It can cause repressive treatment,
When they put the blame on you.

I know now just where I stand,
These thoughts will never cross,
Victim of security,
Hoping to get lost.

Bet you've worked the whole machine,
And never missed out much,
Still staring in the mirror,
Trying so hard not to push.

Put you on a wooden cross,
Nailed reasons to your hand,
Covered in self-pity,

Maybe now you'll understand.

Overcrowding
(written on the reverse of The Only Mistake)

Faces pressed flat against glass windows,
Ten men in a room for two,
Censorship stops here,
No isolation,
Only detoxification.

Abnormal relationships formed,
In corners and on floors,
Breathless, breeding and cramped on all fours
No view, no sense of time.

It was a strange way to go.

Untitled (1980)

Edging towards, a child you may keep,
Retreading the boards pretty young thing
You'll get your reward,
Permission to speak
A place to yourself,
A garden with swings,
Handwritten cards do nothing to ease,
The burden
Where is my release,
Face up to them all,
As they sway side to side,
They put me on show,
Disgusts and rewinds,
To take life away
Was life really there,

No sound, no

Untitled and Unfinished

Avenues all lined with trees,
Edens garden left for thieves,
I looked upon an empty stage,
Where all the young men once had played.

Inroads leading on and on,
Filled with strangers every one,
The   arrived and here to stay,
Look then turn their heads away.

Buildings torn down to the ground,
Replaced by new ones thought more sound,
And as torches glow right thru' the night,
A sacrifice for all that's right.

I looked ahead an empty space,
A lifetimes   erased,

and on the reverse ...

hanging from trees by their necks
typecast forgotten young saviours
lost by their own grace and favours
hinder the paths of

Johnny 23 (1979)

Door slides open,
Johnny laughs
A view from above
Sticks his head

Unseen Lyrics

Out of the window and dries his eyes

I remember a winter sometime ago,
Angular patterns formed deep in the ground
Where someone once stood
White on black,
White on white,
Echoed voices bouncing off the buildings around.

A ramp to the trees and trees all around,
I remember a tear, frozen white on white,
I remember nothing.
A grey saloon,
Johnny sighs,
Winds down the window and stares at the road.

Some things never make sense,
A fear of stepping out,
Crouches shivering in the corner, blanket round your shoulder,
Hot then cold, cold then warm, pulse is racing, slowly racing –
stopped.
I remember nights spent listening to until dawn,
I remember nothing.

Door slowly opens,
Johnny sits on his bed,
Lays down and dies.

GIG LIST

29 May 1977 Electric Circus, Manchester

31 May 1977 Rafters, Manchester

2 June 1977 Newcastle

June/July 1977 Several gigs at the Squat, Manchester

30 June 1977 Rafters, Manchester

3 October 1977 Electric Circus, Manchester

7 October 1977 Salford Technical College

8 October 1977 Manchester Polytechnic

19 October 1977 Pipers Disco, Manchester

December 1977 Rafters, Manchester

New Year's Eve 1977 Swinging Apple, Liverpool (their last gig as Warsaw)

25 January 1978 Pips disco, Manchester (their first gig as Joy Division)

14 March 1978 Bowden Vale Youth Club, Altrincham

28 March 1978 Rafters, Manchester

14 April 1978 Rafters, Manchester

20 May 1978 Mayflower Club, Manchester

9 June 1978 The Factory, Manchester

June 1978 Band on the Wall, Manchester

15 July 1978 Eric's, Liverpool

27 July 1978 Roots Club, Leeds

29 August 1978 Band on the Wall, Manchester

4 September 1978 Band on the Wall, Manchester

9 September 1978 Eric's, Liverpool

10 September 1978 Royal Standard, Bradford

20 September 1978 appeared on Granada TV's *What's On* playing

'Shadowplay'

2 October 1978 Institute of Technology, Bolton

12 October 1978 Kelly's, Manchester

October 1978 Band on the Wall, Manchester

20 October 1978 The Factory, Manchester

24 October 1978 Fan Club, Leeds

4 November 1978 Eric's, Liverpool

14 November 1978 Odeon, Canterbury

15 November 1978 Brunel University, Uxbridge

19 November 1978 Bristol

20 November 1978 Check Inn, Altrincham

26 November 1978 New Electric Circus, Manchester

1 December 1978 The Factory, Manchester

22 December 1978 Revolution Club, York

27 December 1978 Hope and Anchor, London

31 January 1979 recorded first John Peel session

10 February 1979 Bolton.

14 February 1979 transmission of first John Peel session

16 February 1979 Eric's, Liverpool

28 February 1979 Playhouse, Nottingham

1 March 1979 Hope and Anchor, London

4 March 1979 Marquee, London

14 March 1979 Bowden Vale Youth Club, Altrincham

30 March 1979 Youth Centre, Walthamstow, London

3 May 1979 Eric's, Liverpool

11 May 1979 The Factory, Manchester

17 May 1979 Acklam Hall, London

23 May 1979 Bowden Vale, Altrincham

7 June 1979 Fan Club, Leeds

13 June 1979 Russell Club, Manchester

16 June 1979 Odeon, Canterbury

22 June 1979 Good Mood, Halifax

3 July 1979 Free Trade Hall, Manchester

5 July 1979 Limit Club, Sheffield

11 July 1979 Roots Club, Leeds

13 July 1979 The Factory, Manchester
27 July 1979 Imperial Hotel, Blackpool
28 July 1979 Stuff the Superstars Special, Funhouse Festival, Mayflower Club, Manchester
2 August 1979 Prince of Wales Conference Centre, YMCA, Tottenham Court Road, London
8 August 1979 Romulus Club, Birmingham
11 August 1979 Eric's, Liverpool
13 August 1979 Nashville Rooms, London
24 August 1979 Youth Club, Walthamstow, London
27 August 1979 Leigh Festival
31 August 1979 Electric Ballroom, London
8 September 1979 Futurama '79, Queen's Hall, Leeds
15 September 1979 'Transmission' and 'She's Lost Control' broadcast on BBC 2's *Something Else*
22 September 1979 Nashville Rooms, London
28 September 1979 The Factory, Manchester
2 October 1979 Mountford Hall, Liverpool
3 October 1979 Leeds University
4 October 1979 City Hall, Newcastle
5 October 1979 Apollo, Glasgow
6 October 1979 Odeon, Edinburgh
7 October 1979 Capitol, Aberdeen
8 October 1979 Caird Hall, Dundee
16 October 1979 Plan K, Brussels
19 October 1979 Bangor University
20 October 1979 Loughborough University
21 October 1979 Top Rank, Sheffield
22 October 1979 Assembly Rooms, Derby
23 October 1979 King George's Hall, Blackburn
24 October 1979 Odeon, Birmingham
25 October 1979 St George's Hall, Bradford
26 October 1979 Electric Ballroom, London
27 October 1979 Apollo, Manchester
28 October 1979 Apollo, Manchester

29 October 1979 De Montfort Hall, Leicester
30 October 1979 New Theatre, Oxford
1 November 1979 Civic Hall, Guilford
2 November 1979 Winter Gardens, Bournemouth
3 November 1979 Sofia Gardens, Cardiff
4 November 1979 Colston Hall, Bristol
5 November 1979 Pavilion, Hemel Hempstead
7 November 1979 Pavilion, West Runton
9 November 1979 Rainbow Theatre, London
10 November 1979 Rainbow Theatre, London
26 November 1979 recorded second John Peel session
8 December 1979 Eric's, Liverpool, matinée and evening
10 December 1979 transmission of second John Peel session
18 December 1979 Les Bains Douche, Paris (thirty minutes of this
   broadcast on Paris FM radio)
31 December 1979 New Year's Eve party and gig above
   Woolworth's, Oldham Street, Manchester
11 January 1980 Paradiso Club, Amsterdam
12 January 1980 Trojan Horse, The Hague
13 January 1980 Doornrood, Nitjmegen, Netherlands
14 January 1980 King Kong, Antwerp
15 January 1980 The Basement, Cologne
16 January 1980 Lantaren, Rotterdam
17 January 1980 Plan K, Brussels
18 January 1980 Effenaar Club, Eindhoven
19 January 1980 Club Vera, Gronigen
21 January 1980 Kantkino, Berlin
7 February 1980 New Osbourne Club, Manchester
8 February 1980 University College, London
20 February 1980 Town Hall, High Wycombe
28 February 1980 Warehouse, Preston
29 February 1980 Lyceum, London.
5 March 1980 Trinity Hall, Bristol
2 April 1980 Moonlight Club, West Hampstead, London
3 April 1980 Moonlight Club, West Hampstead, London

4 April 1980 Moonlight Club, West Hampstead, London

4 April 1980 Rainbow Theatre, London

5 April 1980 Malvern Winter Gardens

8 April 1980 Derby Hall, Bury

11 April 1980 The Factory, Manchester

19 April 1980 Ajanta Theatre, Derby

2 May 1980 High Hall, Birmingham University

26 June 1980 'Love Will Tear Us Apart' video shown on Granada
TV's *Fun Factory*.

INDEX

Note: Songs and recordings by Joy Division are entered individually; others will be found under the artists' names.

SELECT SOUNDTRACKS

CDs available for Faber and Faber titles

A Life Less Ordinary
Amateur
Apocalypse now
Breaking The Waves

Carrington
Casino
Cinema Paradiso
Crash

Dangerous Liasons
Dead Man Walking
Even Cowgirls Get The Blues
Flirting With Disaster
Flower Of My Secret
From Dusk Til Dawn

The Godfather
Goodfellas
Kids

The Last Temptation
  of Christ
Leaving Las Vegas
Lost Highway
The Madness Of
  King George

Natural Born Killers
Orlando
Pulp Fiction

The Remains
  of The Day
Resevoir Dogs
sex, lies and
  videotape
Suburbia

Taxi Driver
Three Colours Blue
Three Colours Red
Trainspotting
True Romance
The Usual Suspects

and many more...